ITALIAN **DESSERTS** & PASTRIES

ITALIAN
DESSERTS
& PASTRIES

The Taunton Press

The Taunton Press
Inspiration for hands-on living®

The Taunton Press, Inc.
63 South Main Street
PO Box 5506, Newtown, CT 06470-5506
e-mail: tp@taunton.com

Translations:

Contextus s.r.l., Pavia (Sarah Elizabeth Cree) - Catherine Howard -
Salvatore Ciolfi - Mary Doyle - John Venerella - Free z'be, Paris -
Rosetta Translations SARL - Helen Farrell

LIBRARY OF CONGRESS CATALOGING-IN-PUBLICATION DATA IN PROGRESS
ISBN: 978-1-62710-474-6

Printed in China
10 9 8 7 6 5 4 3 2 1

EDITED BY
ACADEMIA BARILLA

INTRODUCTION
GIANLUIGI ZENTI

TEXT
LORENA CARRARA
CHEF MARIO GRAZIA
MARIAGRAZIA VILLA

RECIPES
CHEF MARIO GRAZIA

PHOTOGRAPHS
CHEF MARIO GRAZIA
CHEF STEFANO LODI
CHEF MATTEO MANFERDINI
CHATO MORANDI
ALBERTO ROSSI
LUCIO ROSSI
CHEF LUCA ZANGA

ACADEMIA BARILLA EDITORIAL COORDINATION
CHATO MORANDI
REBECCA PICKRELL
ILARIA ROSSI

GRAPHIC DESIGN
MARIA CUCCHI

CONTENTS

LIST OF RECIPES

A MOTHER'S CARESS

FROM THE AMARETTO COOKIE FROM PIEDMONT AND THE SICILIAN CASSATA TO THE ALTO ADIGE STRUDEL AND ZEPPOLE FROM CAMPANIA, THE LIST OF TRADITIONAL ITALIAN DESSERTS IS AS LONG AS IT IS DELICIOUS. THE RECIPES CHANGE FROM ONE AREA TO THE NEXT, AND MAY BE OF NOBLE OR HUMBLE ORIGIN, BUT THEY ALL HAVE A LOVABLE CHARACTER AND ARE PREPARED WITH GENUINE, TOP-QUALITY INGREDIENTS. THEY ALSO HAVE AN IMPRESSIVE HISTORY BEHIND THEM, STARTING FROM ANCIENT ROME AND CARRIED ON TO THE PRESENT DAY.

IN ITALY, NO ONE HAS EVER RENOUNCED DESSERTS. NOT EVEN OUR ANCESTORS, WHO HAD RATHER STRONG TASTES. EVEN CATO THE CENSOR, FAMOUS FOR HAVING BEEN A PRINCIPLED MAN AND LITTLE INCLINED TO THE PLEASURES OF THE TABLE, LAVISHLY DESCRIBED, IN "DE AGRI CULTURA," A CAKE CALLED "PLACENTA," WHICH HAD A CRUNCHY FLOUR BASE AND, ON TOP, A GENEROUS LAYER OF HONEY CREAM AND FRESH PECORINO, A FORERUNNER OF TODAY'S CHEESECAKE. AND IF AT THE BEGINNING DESSERT HAD A RITUAL SIGNIFICANCE, IN KEEPING WITH THE SPIRITUAL PRINCIPLE THAT THE BEST THINGS SHOULD BE OFFERED TO THE GODS AND NOT KEPT FOR ONESELF, OR WERE USED FOR CELEBRATING SACRED MOMENTS OF TRANSITION IN THE LIFE OF AN INDIVIDUAL OR A COMMUNITY, LIKE BAPTISMS AND WEDDINGS, IT THEN BECAME A DAILY PLEASURE, IDENTIFIED WITH, AS GABRIELE D'ANNUNZIO PUT IT, "THE

ACADEMIA BARILLA

LUXURY OF THE TABLE." FIRST THE ARISTOCRATS, THEN THE MIDDLE CLASSES AND, FINALLY, THE WHOLE POPULATION.

ITALIAN CREATIVITY HAS PRODUCED DESSERTS THAT ARE NOW FAMOUS ALL OVER THE WORLD, LIKE GELATO, NOUGAT, AND TIRAMISÙ, AND THAT HAVE WON EVERYONE OVER WITH THEIR TENDERNESS, ENTHUSIASM, AND WARMTH. BECAUSE SWEETNESS IS AN INTEGRAL PART OF OUR GASTRONOMIC SOUL — IT BRINGS US BACK TO THE JOYS OF CHILDHOOD, TO THE GOODNESS OF A PIECE OF HOMEMADE CAKE, THE SMALL AND COVETED TREAT REPRESENTED BY A COOKIE, THE PLEASURE OF TASTING A CHOCOLATE IN SECRET, THE PRICELESS COMFORT OF A DISH OF PASTRY CREAM, THE CRACKLING FESTIVITY OF FRIED TORTELLI DURING CARNIVAL, WHICH ARE SO TASTY THAT YOU CANNOT STOP AT JUST ONE...

AS DESCRIBED BY THE NINETEENTH-CENTURY ITALIAN PHYSICIAN AND ANTHROPOLOGIST PAOLO MANTEGAZZA, DESSERTS ARE "LIKE A MOTHER'S LOVING CARESS." AND THAT IS WHY WE CANNOT DO WITHOUT THEM.

GIANLUIGI ZENTI
DIRECTOR OF ACADEMIA BARILLA

11

BASIC DESSERT RECIPES

CHAPTER ONE

BUTTERCREAM

CREMA AL BURRO

Preparation time: 15 minutes

Makes about 30 oz. (850 g) of buttercream

3/4 cup plus 2 tbsp. (200 g) **unsalted butter, room temperature**
2 cups (240 g) **confectioners' sugar**
3 cups (360 g) **pastry cream (see p. 16)**
1/3 oz. (10 g) **hazelnut paste**
2 tbsp. plus 2 tsp. (40 ml) **rum**

Method

Using a mixer with a whisk attachment, beat the butter with the confectioners' sugar. Add the pastry cream, then the hazelnut paste and rum. Adjust the flavor by adding hazelnut paste or rum as desired.

CHOCOLATE VARIATION

Make the standard buttercream recipe, facing page, up to the addition of the pastry cream.

Blend 1/3 cup (30 g) unsweetened cocoa powder and 3 ounces (85 g) dark chocolate, finely chopped, with the pastry cream.

PASTRY CREAM
CREMA PASTICCIERA

Preparation time: 15 minutes + 10 minutes cooking time

Makes about 32 oz. (900 g) pastry cream

2 cups (500 ml) **milk**
1 **vanilla bean, split lengthwise, seeds scraped**
4 **large egg yolks**
3/4 cup (150 g) **sugar**
1/3 cup (40 g) **all-purpose flour, sifted**

Method

In a medium saucepan over medium heat, bring the milk and the vanilla bean to a boil.

Meanwhile, beat the egg yolks and sugar in a bowl. Add the flour and mix well.

Remove the vanilla bean and pour a little boiling milk over the egg yolks to temper them, whisking constantly. Whisk in the remainder of the milk.

Return mixture to the saucepan over medium heat and bring to a boil, whisking constantly until the mixture thickens, 5 to 7 minutes.

Transfer the pastry cream to a container and let cool. Refrigerate in an airtight container for up to 3 days.

CHOCOLATE VARIATION

Blend the unsweetened cocoa powder and finely chopped dark chocolate with the boiling pastry cream.

HAZELNUT VARIATION

Mix the base pastry cream with 4 oz. (120 g) of pure hazelnut paste for each 2.2 pounds (1 kg) of pastry cream.

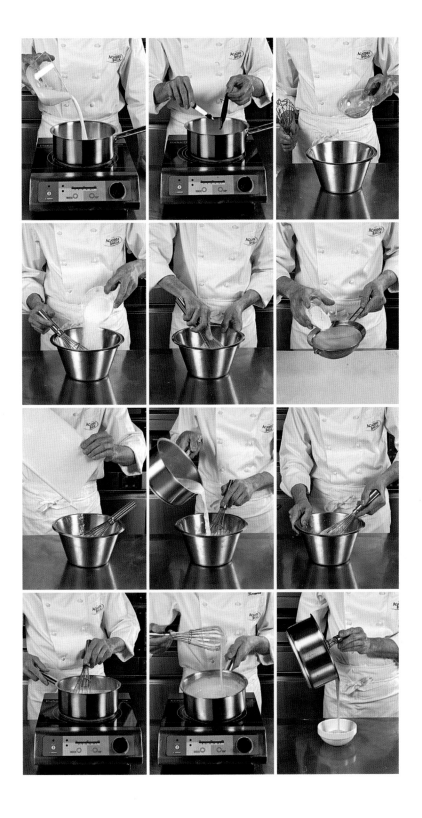

CHOCOLATE GANACHE
GANACHE AL CIOCCOLATO

Preparation time: 10 minutes + 4 hours chilling time

Ingredients for about 7 oz. (200 g)

3 1/2 oz. (100 g) **dark chocolate, finely chopped**
1/2 cup (100 ml) **whipping cream**
2 tsp. (10 ml) **corn syrup (optional)**

Method

Place the chocolate in a bowl.

In a small saucepan, bring the cream to a simmer with the corn syrup, if desired. Pour the cream over the chocolate. Mix gently with a flexible spatula (do not use a whisk; it would add too much air) until the mixture is smooth and velvety.

Transfer ganache to a bowl and chill, covered, stirring occasionally, until thickened but spreadable, about 4 hours.

SPONGE CAKE
PAN DI SPAGNA

Preparation time: 20 minutes + 20 minutes cooking time

Makes two 8-inch (20 cm) round sponge cakes

Unsalted butter, for pans
1 1/2 cups (185 g) all-purpose flour, plus more for pans
5 large eggs
1 cup (200 g) sugar
1 tsp. honey
Zest of ½ lemon, grated
Vanilla extract
3 tbsp. plus 2 1/4 tsp. (30 g) cornstarch

Method

Heat the oven to 350°F (180°C).

Butter and flour two 8-inch (20 cm) cake pans.

In a heatproof bowl set over (not in) a pan of simmering water, gently heat the eggs with the sugar and honey, whisking until the sugar dissolves and the mixture is fluffy. Whisk in the lemon zest and a dash of vanilla.

Sift together the flour and the cornstarch. Add to the egg mixture, using a spatula to gently fold the mixture so that the eggs do not lose volume.

Pour the batter into the pans until two-thirds full. Bake for about 20 minutes, or until tops of cakes are golden brown.

CHOCOLATE SPONGE CAKE

2 tbsp. (30 g) **unsalted butter, melted and cooled to room temperature, plus more for pans**
1 1/8 cups (115 g) **all-purpose flour, plus more for pans**
4 **large eggs**
1/2 cup plus 2 tbsp. (125 g) **sugar**
1/4 cup plus 2 tsp. (25 g) **cocoa powder**
Vanilla extract

Method

Heat the oven to 350°F (175°C).

Butter and flour two 8-inch (20 cm) cake pans.

In a heatproof bowl set over (not in) a pan of simmering water, gently heat the eggs with the sugar, whisking until the sugar dissolves and the mixture is fluffy.

Sift together the flour and cocoa. Add to egg mixture, followed by the butter and a dash of vanilla; mix well.

Pour the batter into the prepared pans until two-thirds full. Bake for about 20 minutes, or until tops of cakes are golden brown.

SHORT PASTRY DOUGH

PASTA FROLLA

Preparation time: 20 minutes + 1 hour resting time

Makes about 2 1/2 pounds (1.2 kilograms)

1 1/3 cups (300 g) unsalted butter, room temperature
1 1/4 cups (250 g) sugar
Salt
2 large eggs plus 1 egg yolk
Vanilla extract
4 cups (500 g) all-purpose flour
1 tsp. (3 g) baking powder (optional)
Vegetable oil, for plastic wrap

Method

On a lightly floured surface or with an electric mixer, cream the butter with the sugar, then mix in a pinch of salt, the eggs, egg yolk, and dash of vanilla.

Sift together the flour and baking powder, if using. Add to the butter mixture, then knead briefly until you have a smooth, uniform dough.

Wrap dough in lightly oiled plastic wrap. Refrigerate for at least 1 hour before using.

CHOCOLATE SHORT PASTRY DOUGH

1 1/4 cups (300 g) **unsalted butter, room temperature**
1 1/4 cups (250 g) **sugar**
Salt
1 **large egg plus 3 egg yolks**
Vanilla extract
4 cups (500 g) **all-purpose flour**
1/4 cup plus 2 tsp. (25 g) **unsweetened cocoa powder**
1 tsp. (3 g) baking powder (optional)
Vegetable oil, for plastic wrap

Method

On a lightly floured surface or with an electric mixer, cream the butter with the sugar, then mix in a pinch of salt, eggs, egg yolks, and dash of vanilla.

Sift together the flour, cocoa, and baking powder, if using. Add to the butter mixture, then knead briefly until you have a smooth, uniform dough.

Wrap dough in lightly oiled plastic wrap. Refrigerate for at least 1 hour before using.

CREAM PUFF PASTRY DOUGH
PASTA PER BIGNÈ

Preparation time: 25 minutes + 20 minutes cooking time

Makes about 50 cream puffs

1/2 cup (100 ml) **water**
3 1/2 tbsp. (50 g) **cold unsalted butter, cut into small pieces, plus more for baking sheet**
1/4 tsp. (1 g) **salt**
1/2 cup (60 g) **all-purpose flour, sifted**
2 **large eggs**

Method

Heat oven to 375°F (190°C).

In a saucepan, bring the water to a boil with the butter and salt. Add the flour all at once to the boiling water and whisk. When the mixture begins to thicken, stir with a wooden spoon and continue cooking over medium heat for 2 to 3 minutes, until the dough pulls away from the sides of the pan.

Remove from the heat, let cool slightly, then add the eggs, one at a time, incorporating each before adding the next.

Use a pastry bag fitted with a 1/4-inch (6 mm) tip to pipe cream puffs onto a buttered (or parchment-lined) baking sheet.

Bake for 10 minutes, then open oven door slightly and bake for an additional 10 minutes, until puffs are golden brown.

PUFF PASTRY DOUGH

PASTA SFOGLIA

Preparation time: 40 minutes + 1 hour 20 minutes chilling time

Makes about 2 1/2 pounds (1.2 kilograms)

FOR THE BUTTER MIXTURE
2 1/4 cups (500 g) **unsalted butter, room temperature**
1 1/4 cups (150 g) **all-purpose flour, plus more for dusting**

FOR THE DOUGH
2 3/4 cups (350 g) **all-purpose flour, plus more for dusting**
1 1/2 tsp. (10 g) **salt**
3/4 cup (180 ml) **water**

Method

For the butter mixture: Knead the butter and flour on a clean, lightly floured surface (or a pastry board). Sandwich the butter mixture between two sheets of parchment or wax paper. Flatten with a rolling pin as evenly as possible to form a rectangle. Transfer to a baking sheet (without removing the paper) and refrigerate while you make the dough (for at least 30 minutes).

For the dough: Combine the flour, salt, and water on a clean work surface, mixing the ingredients with your hands until you have a smooth dough, about 1 minute. Shape into a ball and refrigerate for at least 20 minutes.

On a clean, lightly floured surface, roll out the dough into a rectangle. Remove the top layer of paper from the butter and invert the butter in the center of the dough so it forms a diamond shape. Remove the other layer of paper. Fold the corners of the dough over the butter, like an envelope, covering it completely. Transfer to the baking sheet, cover, and refrigerate for 30 minutes.

CAKES AND TARTS

CHAPTER TWO

MERINGUE CAKE WITH CREAM
MERINGATA ALLA PANNA

Preparation time: 30 minutes + 3 hours cooking time

4 to 6 Servings

FOR THE SYRUP
2 tbsp. (30 ml) **water**
1/3 cup plus 1 tbsp. (80 g) **sugar**
2 3/4 tbsp. (40 ml) **maraschino cherry liqueur**

FOR THE MERINGUE ROUNDS
5 large (100 g) **egg whites**
1 cup (200 g) **sugar**
2 tbsp. plus 1 1/2 tsp. (20 g) **cornstarch (optional)**

FOR THE LAYERS
9 oz. (250 g) **chocolate pastry cream (see p. 16)**
One 8-inch (20 cm) **round sponge cake (see p. 20)**
1 3/4 cups (200 g) **sweetened whipped cream**
1 cup (125 g) **fresh raspberries**

FOR DUSTING
Confectioners' sugar
Unsweetened cocoa powder

Method

For the syrup: Bring the water and sugar to a boil in a saucepan. Let the syrup cool, then combine it with the maraschino liqueur.

Heat the oven to 200°F (100°C).

For the meringue rounds: Beat the egg whites and 1/4 cup of sugar until the egg whites form stiff, glossy peaks. Gently fold in the remaining 3/4 cup of sugar (mixed with the cornstarch, if using). Use a pastry bag fitted with a plain 3/4 inch (18 to 20 mm) tip to pipe two meringue rounds, about 8 inches (20 cm) in diameter, onto a parchment-lined baking sheet.

Bake the meringues, leaving the oven door slightly open, for about 3 hours. Let cool. Store the meringue disks in a dry place until ready to use (you can keep them in an airtight tin for up to 2 weeks, or frozen for a month).

Soak the sponge cake with the syrup, using a brush.

Spread the pastry cream over the first round, then place the sponge cake on top. Pour syrup over this layer and cover with the whipped cream, reserving some for the garnish.

Arrange a few raspberries on top and cover with the second meringue round.

Garnish the border with the remaining whipped cream and raspberries. Dust with confectioners' sugar and cocoa.

Difficulty

MILLEFEUILLE
MILLEFOGLIE

Preparation time: 30 minutes + 3 hours cooking time

4 to 6 Servings

FOR THE SUGAR FONDANT
5 tsp. (25 ml) **water**
1/2 cup plus 2 tbsp. (125 g) **sugar**
4 tsp. (20 ml) **corn syrup**

FOR THE CAKE
11 oz. (300 g) **puff pastry dough**
(see p. 26)
9 oz. (250 g) **chocolate pastry cream**
(see p. 16)
9 oz. (250 g) **hazelnut pastry cream**
(see p. 16)

FOR DUSTING
Confectioners' sugar
Cocoa powder

Difficulty

Method

For the fondant: Combine the water, sugar, and corn syrup in a saucepan (preferably copper) over medium-high heat. Cook the syrup, without stirring, until it reaches 240°F (115°C) on a candy thermometer.

Pour the syrup onto a slightly damp marble surface (or a baking sheet). Let sit at room temperature for 5 minutes, then, using a wooden spatula, work the fondant until it becomes opaque and creamy.

With moistened hands, knead the fondant into a ball, as you would bread dough, until it is smooth. Wrap fondant in plastic wrap and place in an airtight container until ready to use.

Roll out the puff pastry dough to between 1/10 inch (3 mm) and 1/16 inch (2 mm) thick. Pierce with the tines of a fork and let rest for about 30 minutes, to ensure it does not lose its shape during baking.

Heat the oven to 350°F (180°C). Line a baking sheet with parchment.

Cut 3 rounds of equal size from the dough and bake on parchment-lined baking sheet for about 15 minutes. Just before disks are done baking, dust them with confectioners' sugar and—either by increasing oven temperature to 500°F (260°C) or placing disks under the broiler—bake until sugar caramelizes.

Remove from the oven and let cool.

Use a pastry bag fitted with a plain tip to pipe the chocolate pastry cream over the first round. Place the second round on top and cover it with hazelnut cream.

Cover the dessert with the final puff pastry round.

In a bain-marie (hot-water bath) or microwave, gently heat the fondant until it liquefies and spread it onto the last pastry round. To decorate the surface, color a small amount of the sugar fondant with cocoa and drizzle it over the surface.

MIXED BERRY CAKE

TORTA AI FRUTTI DI BOSCO

Preparation time: 30 minutes + 1 hour cooling time

6 Servings

FOR THE SYRUP

2 tbsp. (30 ml) **water**

1/3 cup plus 1 tbsp. (80 g) **sugar**

2 3/4 tbsp. (40 ml) **maraschino cherry liqueur**

FOR THE CAKE

11 oz. (300g) **pastry cream (see p. 16)**

2 **gelatin sheets, softened in cold water and squeezed dry**

5 cups (300 g) **sweetened whipped cream**

One 7-inch (18 cm) **round baked chocolate short pastry (see p. 23)**

9 oz. (250 g) **mixed berries and strawberries**

One 7-inch (18 cm) **round sponge cake (see p. 20), weighing 3 oz. (80 g)**

1/3 cup (40 g) **pistachio nuts, chopped**

FOR GARNISH

Fresh mint leaves

Confectioners' sugar

Method

For the syrup: Bring the water and sugar to a boil in a saucepan over medium-high heat. Let cool, then add the maraschino liqueur.

For the cake: Heat 2 tablespoons of pastry cream in a small pan, add the gelatin sheets, and let dissolve completely.

Remove from the heat and add the remaining cold pastry cream, then gently incorporate half of the sweetened whipped cream.

Spread two-thirds of the pastry cream mixture on the layer of chocolate short pastry, sprinkling some of the berries on top. Soak the sponge cake layer with the maraschino syrup. Place on top of berries and short pastry layer. Spread the whole with the remaining pastry cream.

To simplify the assembly of the dessert, you can put it together inside a round metal dessert mold, removing it once the dessert is complete.

Cover the sides with the pistachios. Refrigerate the cake until it is set, about 1 hour.

When the cake is set, use a pastry bag fitted with a plain tip to pipe the remaining whipped cream in a border around the top of the cake. Arrange the remaining berries and strawberries on top, and garnish with a few fresh mint leaves and a dusting of confectioners' sugar.

Difficulty

TRUFFLE CAKE
TORTA TARTUFATA

Preparation time: 30 minutes + 12 hours resting time

6 Servings

FOR THE CHOCOLATE COATING
7 oz. (200 g) **dark chocolate**
1 1/2 oz. (40 g) **hazelnut paste**
2 tbsp. (30 ml) **milk, room temperature**

FOR THE SYRUP
1/3 cup plus 1 tbsp. (80 g) **sugar**
8 tsp. (40 ml) **rum or orange-flavored liqueur**
One 7-inch (18 cm) **round sponge cake (see p. 20)**, weighing 11 oz. (300 g)
11 oz. (300 g) **chocolate buttercream (see p. 15)**

FOR DUSTING
Confectioners' sugar

Difficulty

Method

For the chocolate coating: Melt the chocolate in a microwave or in a bowl set over (not in) simmering water and mix it with the hazelnut paste and milk. Pour onto a baking sheet to temper and let set overnight.

For the syrup: Bring the water and sugar to a boil in a saucepan over medium-high heat. Let cool, then add the liqueur or rum.

With a serrated knife, slice the sponge cake into three even layers. Soak one layer of cake with the syrup, using a brush. Spread about one-third of the chocolate buttercream on the first cake layer. Repeat with the remaining two layers.

Place the chocolate on a nonstick work surface and roll out with a rolling pin to between 1/16 and 1/32 inch (1 mm) thick. For thinner sheets of chocolate, you can use a pasta machine to roll the chocolate out (thin it out a little with the rolling pin before running it through), with the control turned to the thinnest setting. Dust your work surface, rolling pin or pasta machine rollers very lightly with confectioners' sugar to keep the chocolate from sticking.

Cover the sides and top of the cake with the resulting sheet of chocolate. Before serving, dust cake with confectioners' sugar.

Chocolate Desserts

How many chocolate cakes are there? A lot! From the simplest cocoa sponge cake (perfect for breakfast), to the most elaborate truffle cake and the most traditional, like the velvety Italian chocolate cake known as tenerina *cake or* torta cioccolatina, *truly a food of the gods.... Then there are the unique variations, like chocolate–zucchini cake, and the light varieties, like puffed-rice chocolate cake, and the most caloric ones, like the divine chocolate, coffee, and mascarpone cheesecake. Every one of them is rich in flavor and loved by children and adults alike.*

CHOCOLATE CAKE WITH WHIPPED CREAM AND CHERRIES

TORTA AL CIOCCOLATO CON PANNA E AMARENE

Preparation time: 2 hours 15 minutes + 1 hour cooling time

6 Servings

FOR THE CHOCOLATE SPONGE CAKE

3 large eggs
1/3 cup plus 1 tbsp.(80 g) **sugar**
3/8 cup (50 g) **all-purpose flour,
  plus more for pan**
2 tbsp. (10 g) **unsweetened cocoa powder**
2 tbsp. (15 g) **cornstarch**
1/2 tsp. (3 ml) **vanilla extract**
1/2 tsp. (2 g) **baking powder (optional)**
2 tsp. (10 g) **unsalted butter, melted,
  plus more for pan**

FOR THE FILLING

1/4 cup (30 g) **cornstarch**
3/4 cup (150 g) **sugar**
9 oz. (250 g) **pitted cherries**
Juice of half a lemon
5 cups (300 g) **sweetened whipped cream**

FOR THE SYRUP

1/3 cup plus 1 tbsp. (80 g) **sugar**
2 tbsp. (30 ml) **water**
2 1/2 tbsp. (35 ml) **maraschino liqueur**

FOR THE TOPPING

Milk chocolate bar
Confectioners' sugar

Difficulty

Method

Heat the oven to 350°F (180°C).

For the sponge cake: Heat the eggs and sugar in a bowl set over (not in) simmering water, stirring with a whisk. Beat the mixure (preferably with an electric mixer) until fluffy. With a spatula, fold in the flour, cocoa, cornstarch, a dash of vanilla, and the baking powder. Add the melted butter.

Butter and flour a 9-by-13-inch cake pan. Pour the filling into the pan two-thirds full. Bake for 20 to 25 minutes, or until it is golden brown. Invert the cake onto a wire rack to cool.

For the filling: Mix the cornstarch with the sugar and combine it with the cherries in a saucepan. Bring to a boil over medium-high heat and let boil for 1 to 2 minutes. Add the lemon juice. Let it cool completely.

For the maraschino syrup: Bring the sugar and water to a boil in a saucepan over medium-high heat. Let it cool, then add the liqueur. For this recipe, you will need about 3/8 cup (100 ml) of syrup.

Using a serrated knife, slice the cake into two layers. Soak the bottom layer with the syrup. Cover it with the cherry filling. Spread with a layer of whipped cream. Put the second layer of sponge cake on top. Soak with the syrup, then completely cover the surface and edges of the cake with the remaining whipped cream.

Garnish with chocolate shavings, if desired. (To make shavings, scrape a chocolate bar with a knife held perpendicular to it.) Refrigerate the cake for at least 1 hour.

Sprinkle with confectioners' sugar before serving.

JAM TART

CROSTATA ALLA CONFETTURA

Preparation time: 25 minutes + 20 to 25 minutes cooking time

4 to 6 Servings

11 oz. (300 g) **short pastry dough (see p. 22)**
3/4 cup plus 1 1/2 tsp. (250 g) **jam (any flavor)**

Method

Heat the oven to 350°F (180°C).

On a clean, lightly floured work surface, roll out the pastry dough to a thickness of about 1/10 inch (3 mm). Fit into an 8-inch (20 cm) tart pan, trimming dough around the edges of the pan.

Spread the pan with a layer of jam.

Cut the remaining short pastry dough into shapes of your choice (such as leaves or half-moons) and decorate the surface of the tart.

Bake for about 20 to 25 minutes.

Let the jam tart cool completely before removing it from the pan.

Difficulty

LEMON CREAM TART

CROSTATA CON CREMA AL LIMONE

Preparation time: 30 minutes + 20 minutes cooking time + 2 hours resting time

4 to 6 Servings

All-purpose flour, for dusting

9 oz. (250 g) **short pastry dough (see p. 22)**

FOR THE FILLING

Zest of 2 **lemons**

Juice of 2 **lemons (1/4 cup plus 1 tsp., or 65 ml, of juice)**

3/4 cup plus 2 tsp. (180 g) **unsalted butter, room temperature**

3/4 cup (150 g) **sugar**

7 **large egg yolks**

3/4 cup plus 4 tsp. (100 g) **confectioners' sugar, plus more for dusting**

1/3 cup plus 1 tbsp. (80 g) **cornstarch, sifted**

Method

Heat the oven to 350°F (180°C).

On a clean, lightly floured work surface, roll out the pastry dough to a thickness of about 1/10 inch (3 mm) thick. Fit into an 8-inch (20 cm) tart pan, trimming the dough around the edges of the pan. Bake for about 20 minutes.

Bring the lemon zest and juice to a boil with the butter and sugar.

Beat the egg yolks with the confectioners' sugar. Add the cornstarch to the egg mixture. Add this mixture to the lemon juice mixture and bring to a boil, mixing well.

Let the lemon cream cool quickly by pouring it into an ovenproof dish and stirring occasionally.

Fill the baked pastry crust with the lemon cream and let set in the refrigerator for about 2 hours. Before serving, decorate the tart with a dusting of confectioners' sugar.

Not Forgetting Lemon Delight

Just as typical of Italian cuisine is Lemon Delight, a Neapolitan culinary classic. Created in 1978 by Carmine Marzuillo, a pastry chef from the Amalfi Coast, this dessert is made of a sponge cake base soaked in limoncello syrup and filled with a tasty, aromatic lemon cream. Lemon Delight is often served topped with wild strawberries.

Difficulty

BLUEBERRY TART
DOLCE FREDDO AI MIRTILLI NERI

Preparation time: 30 minutes + 10 minutes cooking time

6 Servings

All-purpose flour, for dusting
9 oz. (250 g) short pastry dough
   (see p. 22)

FOR THE FILLING
7/8 cup (2 dl) sweet white wine
2 cups (300 g) fresh blueberries
8 sheets (20 g) gelatin, or 2 envelopes
   (1/2 oz.) granulated gelatin
Butter, for pans
1 cup (200 g) sugar
1/2 tsp. (3 ml) vanilla extract
18 oz. (500 g) ricotta cheese
7 oz. (200 g) whipped cream
1/3 cup (50 g) almonds, peeled

Method

In a saucepan, bring the wine to a boil over medium heat. Add the blueberries and blanch them, stirring constantly, for 30 seconds. Drain and set the blueberries aside. Discard the wine.

Put the gelatin sheets in cold water and leave to soak.

Heat the oven to 350°F (180°C).

Butter a 9-inch (23 cm) tart pan. On a clean, lightly floured work surface, roll out the short pastry dough into a round. Fit into the prepared tart pan, trimming the dough around the edges of the pan and piercing the bottom all over. Bake for 10 to 12 minutes, or until golden. Let cool.

In a large bowl, blend the sugar and a dash of vanilla into the ricotta, stirring until it is smooth and creamy. Stir in the whipped cream, and then the blueberries.

Wring out the gelatin sheets, then heat them in a double boiler or in the microwave until they dissolve. Add the gelatin to the cream mixture.

Pour the filling into the crust and refrigerate until ready to serve.

Serve cold, sprinkled with almonds.

Difficulty

PUMPKIN ALMOND TART
CROSTATA CON ZUCCA E MANDORLE

Preparation time: 45 minutes + 25 to 30 minutes cooking time

4 Servings

FOR THE FILLING

All-purpose flour, for dusting
9 oz. (250 g) **short pastry dough (see p. 22)**
1 lb. (500 g) **whole pumpkin**
2 **large egg yolks**
1/3 cup plus 1 tbsp. (80 g) **sugar**
5 1/2 tsp. (15 g) **cornstarch**
1/2 cup (200 ml) **heavy cream**
1/2 **vanilla bean**
Zest of 1/2 **lemon, grated**
2/3 cup (100 g) **slivered almonds**
Confectioners' sugar

Method

Heat the oven to 350°F (180°C).

Wash the pumpkin, cut it into pieces, and place in a baking pan. Bake for about 30 minutes, or until tender. If the pumpkin begins to brown too quickly, cover it with aluminum foil. Let it cool completely.

Remove the seeds and fibers from the pumpkin, then scoop out the cooked flesh, discarding the peel. Run the pumpkin through a ricer or purée in a food processor.

In a bowl, whisk together the egg yolks with the sugar, then whisk in the cornstarch.

In a small saucepan, bring the cream and the vanilla bean to a boil over medium heat. Pour it in a slow stream over the egg yolk mixture, whisking to combine. Return the mixture to the saucepan and cook over medium, whisking constantly, until a custard forms, about 3 minutes.

Remove custard from heat, discard vanilla pod, and let custard cool.

Add the pumpkin and lemon zest to the custard.

On a clean, lightly floured work surface, roll out the short pastry dough to 1/10 inch (3 mm) thick. Fit into an 8-inch (20 cm) tart pan, trimming the dough around the edges of pan.

Pour the pumpkin filling into the crust. Bake at 350°F (180°C) for about 30 minutes, or until golden brown. Let cool completely before removing the tart from the pan.

Before serving, sprinkle the surface of the tart with the almonds and dust generously with confectioners' sugar.

Difficulty

CHERRY MERINGUE TART
CROSTATA DI CILIEGIE MERINGATA

Preparation time: 50 minutes + 20 minutes cooking time + 1 hour resting time

4 Servings

All-purpose flour, for dusting
9 oz. (250 g) **chocolate short pastry dough (see p. 23)**

FOR THE FILLING
1/3 cup plus 2 tsp. (75 g) **sugar**
1/3 cup plus 1 tsp. (45 g) **cornstarch**
2 1/2 cups (375 g) **pitted cherries**
Juice of 1/2 **lemon**

FOR THE ITALIAN MERINGUE
2 tbsp. (30 ml) **water**
1/2 cup plus 2 tbsp. (125 g) **sugar**
2 **large egg whites**

Method

Heat the oven to 350°F (180°C).

On a clean, lightly floured work surface, roll out the short pastry dough to 1/10 inch (3 mm) thick. Fit into an 8-inch (20 cm) tart pan, trimming the dough around the edges of the pan. Bake the dough for about 15 to 20 minutes, until golden brown.

Combine the sugar and the cornstarch in a small bowl.

In a saucepan over medium heat, bring the cherries and lemon juice to a boil. Add the sugar mixture to the cherries. Cook for 3 minutes, then let cool.

Fill the baked crust with the cherry mixture and refrigerate to let the cherries set.

For the Italian meringue: Heat the water and 1/2 cup plus 2 tsp. (110 g) of the sugar in a saucepan (preferably copper). Meanwhile, with an electric mixer on medium-high speed, beat the egg whites with the remaining 3 1/2 tsp. (15 g) of sugar until stiff peaks form.

When the sugar mixture reaches 250°F (121°C) on a candy thermometer, pour it in a thin stream into the egg whites and beat until cool.

Use a pastry bag fitted with a plain tip to pipe the meringue onto the surface of the tart. (Or simply spread meringue on the tart with a spatula.) To brown the meringue, use a kitchen torch or set the tart briefly under the oven broiler.

Difficulty

MIXED NUT TART
CROSTATA DI FRUTTA SECCA

Preparation time: 35 minutes + 25 minutes cooking time

4 to 6 Servings

9 oz. (250 g) **short pastry dough (see p. 22)**

FOR THE FILLING

1/4 cup (30 g) **hazelnuts**
1/3 cup (30 g) **walnuts**
1/4 cup (30 g) **almonds**
1/4 cup (30 g) **pine nuts**
1/4 cup (30 g) **pistachio nuts**
3/4 cup (150 g) **sugar**
4 tsp. (10 g) **all-purpose flour, plus more for dusting**
1 **vanilla bean**
1 **large egg**

FOR THE TOPPING

4 1/4 oz. (120 g) **assorted nuts**
7 1/2 tsp. (50 g) **apricot jelly**

Method

Using a food processor, pulse the nuts and sugar until finely ground. Mix the ground nuts with the flour.

With a sharp knife, slice the vanilla bean lengthwise and scrape out the seeds, adding them to the nut mixture. Add the egg and stir to combine.

Heat the oven to 350°F (180°C).

On a clean, lightly floured work surface, roll out the short pastry dough to 1/10 inch (3 mm) thick. Fit into an 8-inch (20 cm) tart pan, trimming the dough around the edges of the pan.

Fill the dough three-quarters full with the nut mixture. Bake for about 25 minutes or until golden brown.

Let the tart cool, then remove it from the pan and top it with assorted nuts.

In a saucepan, heat the apricot jelly over medium until warmed through. Brush jelly over the nuts to form a glaze.

Difficulty

GENOESE CHRISTMAS CAKE
PANETTONE GENOVESE

Preparation time: 30 minutes + 1 hour cooking time

4 Servings

1 1/3 cups (170 g) **all-purpose flour**
1 1/2 tsp. (5 g) **baking powder**
Salt
1/4 cup plus 1 3/4 tsp. (65 g) **unsalted butter, room temperature**
1/3 cup plus 3/4 tsp. (65 g) **sugar**
1 **large egg**
3 tbsp. plus 2 tsp. (20 g) **pine nuts**
1 oz. (25 g) **candied mixed fruit and candied cherries, diced**
1/4 cup (30 g) **hazelnuts, chopped**
1/3 cup (50 g) **raisins, softened in warm water for 15 minutes, then squeezed of excess moisture**

Method

Heat the oven to 325°F (170°C).

Sift together the flour, baking powder, and a pinch of salt in a bowl. With an electric mixer on medium-high, cream the butter and sugar in another bowl. Add the egg to the butter mixture, then add the flour mixture and stir to combine.

Add the pine nuts, candied fruit and candied cherries, hazelnuts, and raisins; stir just to combine. Do not overwork the batter.

Form the batter into a ball, flatten it slightly, and place it on parchment-lined baking sheet.

Bake for 50 to 60 minutes, or until golden brown.

Pine Nuts Are Good for Love

There are about twenty species of pine that produce the pine nuts used in cooking (those nuts big enough to justify cultivating them as food). In Europe, there are two types of pine tree that produce large pine nuts: the common pine, Pinus pinea, *and the Swiss stone pine,* Pinus cembra. *Extraordinarily rich in protein and antioxidants and high in energy, pine nuts have been consumed since prehistoric times. And since antiquity, they have been celebrated for their aphrodisiacal properties: the Latin poet Ovid, in his* Ars Amatoria, *considered them one of the few foods that could improve romantic capacity. In ancient Greece, pinecones, which conceal the pine nuts wrapped in a protective hull called a strobilus, symbolized the male sexual organ and induced fertility.*

Difficulty

NEAPOLITAN EASTER CAKE
PASTIERA NAPOLETANA

Preparation time: 50 minutes + 1 hour resting time + 40 minutes cooking time

4 Servings

FOR THE CRUST

7 tbsp. (100 g) **unsalted butter, room temperature**

1/2 cup (100 g) **sugar**

1 **large egg**

Zest of 1 **lemon, grated**

Salt

1 1/2 cups (200 g) **all-purpose flour or Italian "00" type flour, plus more for dusting**

1/2 tsp. (2 g) **baking powder**

FOR THE FILLING

8 3/4 oz. (250 g) **ricotta**

3/4 cup (75 g) **confectioners' sugar**

1 cup (225 g) **pastry cream (see p. 16)**

1 **large egg yolk**

5 1/3 oz. (150 g) **"grano cotto per pastiera" (special cooked wheat for pastiera, available in Italian specialty stores and online) or cooked pearl barley**

1 3/4 oz. (50 g) **candied citron, diced**

Orange blossom water (or finely grated orange zest), as needed

Difficulty

Method

For the crust: In a food processor, pulse butter and sugar together. Add the egg, lemon zest, and a pinch of salt and pulse until crumbs form. Sift together the flour and baking powder and pulse with butter mixture until small crumbs form. Transfer to work surface and knead until dough is smooth.

Form into 2 balls, 1 larger than the other, then wrap tightly in plastic and refrigerate for at least 1 hour.

On a lightly floured surface, roll out larger ball to 1/10 inch (3 mm) thick. Fit into a 11-inch (28 cm) springform pan, trimming the dough around the edges of the pan.

For the filling: Press the ricotta through a sieve into a bowl and add the confectioners' sugar, pastry cream, egg yolk, cooked wheat, citron, and orange blossom water. Stir well. Pour the filling into the crust.

Heat oven to 350°F (180°C).

On a lightly floured surface, roll out the smaller dough to about 1/10 inch (3 mm) thick. Cut into 10 1/2-inch-wide strips. Form lattice by placing 5 strips across the top of the pie and the remaining strips at right angles to the firs strips. Trim the strips even with the crust edge; pinch to seal.

Bake for about 1 1/2 hours, or until golden brown.

Let the cake cool completely before removing it from pan. Dust with confectioners' sugar before serving.

WHITE CHOCOLATE AND RASPBERRY TART
CROSTATA AL CIOCCOLATO BIANCO E LAMPONI

Preparation time: 1 hour 5 minutes + 2 hours resting time + 18 to 20 minutes cooking time

4 Servings

FOR THE CHOCOLATE SHORTBREAD CRUST
1 1/2 sticks (95 g) **unsalted butter, room temperature, plus more for pan**
1/4 cup plus 2 tbsp. (85 g) **sugar**
Salt
2 **large egg yolks**
1/2 tsp. (3 ml) **vanilla extract**
1 1/4 cups (165 g) **all-purpose flour, plus more for dusting**
1/4 tsp. (1 g) **baking powder**
2 tbsp. plus 1 tsp. (9 g) **unsweetened cocoa powder**
Vegetable oil, for plastic wrap

FOR THE FILLING
3 oz. (80 g) **raspberry jam**
7 oz. (200 g) **white chocolate, chopped**
3/8 cup (100 ml) **heavy cream**
2 tsp. (10 ml) **light corn syrup**

FOR THE TOPPING
9 oz. (250 g) **fresh raspberries**
Confectioners' sugar

Method

For the crust: With an electric mixer, cream the butter and sugar, then stir in a pinch of salt, the egg yolks, and the vanilla. Sift together the flour, baking powder, and cocoa; add to the butter mixture, then knead briefly until you have a smooth dough. Form the dough into a disk. Wrap the disk in lightly oiled plastic wrap and refrigerate for 1 hour.

Heat the oven to 360°F (180°C).

Butter and flour an 8-inch (20 cm) tart pan with a removable bottom. On a clean, lightly floured work surface, roll out the dough to 1/10 inch (3 mm) thick. Fit into tart pan, trimming dough around edges of pan.

Spread with raspberry jam and bake for 18 to 20 minutes. Transfer the tart pan to a wire rack to cool. Remove the tart shell from the pan.

Place the chocolate in a heatproof bowl. Bring the cream and the corn syrup to a boil in a saucepan and pour it over the chocolate. Mix until you have a smooth, velvety cream. Let cool and pour into the tart shell (it should reach the brim). Top with raspberries and refrigerate for at least 1 hour.

Sprinkle with confectioners' sugar before serving.

Difficulty

PINE NUT CAKE
TORTA AI PINOLI

Preparation time: 30 minutes + 25 minutes cooking time

4 to 6 Servings

FOR THE FILLING
1/4 cup (30 g) **almonds**
2 tbsp. plus 2 tsp. (20 g) **pine nuts**
1/4 cup (50 g) **sugar**
3 1/2 tbsp. (50 g) **unsalted butter, room temperature**
4 tsp. (10 g) **all-purpose flour, plus more for dusting**
1 **large egg**
2 1/2 oz. (70 g) **pastry cream (see p. 16)**
2 tsp. (10 ml) **rum**

FOR THE TOPPING
1/3 cup plus 2 tsp. (50 g) **pine nuts**
Confectioners' sugar

Difficulty

Method

Heat the oven to 350°F (180° C).

For the filling: In a food processor, pulse the almonds, pine nuts, and sugar until finely ground.

In a bowl, stir together the butter with the pine nut mixture. Mix in the flour and then the egg. Finally, add the pastry cream and rum and stir to combine.

On a clean, lightly floured work surface, roll out the pastry dough to about 1/10 inch (3 mm) thick. Line an 8-inch (20 cm) round cake pan with parchment paper. Pour the filling into the prepared pan to two-thirds full.

Cover with pine nuts, dust lightly with confectioners' sugar, and bake for about 25 minutes, or until a cake tester inserted in the middle comes out clean.

Let the cake cool, remove it from the pan, and dust it with confectioners' sugar.

Sweet Rum

Known since antiquity (albeit by a different name), rum is a spirit made by distilling sugarcane molasses. Since rum as we know it today was first distilled (using Indian sugarcane) in London around the fifteenth century, its name might be derived from the first three letters of the word rumble, or from the last three letters of the scientific name for sugarcane: Saccharum officinarum. *Thanks to its full-bodied taste and intense, fruity aroma, rum is used to flavor many traditional Italian desserts.*

MARGHERITA CAKE
TORTA MARGHERITA

Preparation time: 30 minutes + 30 minutes cooking time

6 Servings

3 1/2 tbsp. (50 g) **butter, room temperature, plus more for pan**
1 cup (200 g) **sugar**
3 **large whole eggs plus** 7 **egg yolks**
Zest of 1 **lemon, grated**
1 1/3 cup (150 g) **all-purpose flour, sifted, plus more for pan**
1/3 cup plus 1 tbsp. (50 g) **cornstarch**
1/2 tsp. (3 ml) **vanilla extract**
Confectioners' sugar

Method

Butter and flour an 8-inch (20 cm) round cake pan. Set aside

Melt the butter in a pan set over (not in) simmering water. Remove from heat and let cool.

Whisk together the sugar, eggs, and egg yolks in a bowl until fluffy. Add the lemon zest and, with a spatula, gently fold in the flour, cornstarch, and a dash of vanilla.

Add the butter and mix gently.

Pour the batter into the prepared pan to two-thirds full.

Bake for about 30 minutes, or until a cake tester inserted in the middle comes out clean.

Difficulty

CARROT CAKE
TORTA DI CAROTE

Preparation time: 30 minutes + 35 minutes cooking time

4 o 6 Servings

FOR THE DOUGH

2/3 stick (75 g) **unsalted butter, room temperature, plus more for pan**

3/4 cup (90 g) **all-purpose flour, plus more for pan**

2 tsp. (7 g) **baking powder**

1/3 cup plus 2 tsp. (75 g) **sugar**

2 **large eggs, separated**

5 tsp. (25 ml) **milk**

1/2 cup (50 g) **whole almonds, chopped**

1 1/4 cups (130 g) **grated carrots**

Zest of 1/2 **lemon, grated**

FOR THE TOPPING

Confectioners' sugar

Almond paste

Method

Heat the oven to 325°F (170°C).

Butter and flour an 8-inch (20 cm) round cake pan.

Whisk together the flour and baking powder and set aside.

With an electric mixer on medium, cream the butter with one-third of the sugar.

A bit at a time, alternate adding the yolks, milk, and flour mixture to the butter mixture, stirring to combine after each addition.

Add the almonds, carrots, and lemon zest.

Beat the egg whites with the remaining sugar until stiff peaks form, then fold into the batter. Pour into the prepared pan and bake for about 35 minutes, or until a cake tester inserted in the middle comes out clean.

Let cool, dust with confectioners' sugar, and decorate (here are carrots made with almond paste).

A Sweet Trick for Getting Kids to Eat Carrots

Carrot cake is simple and quick to make and especially loved by children. It is therefore a great way for getting them to try a nourishing, vitamin-packed food like carrots. Thanks to its mild flavor and soft texture, it is good for breakfast or an afternoon snack. There are many excellent variations on the theme, ranging from one that combines apples and carrots to another in which yogurt is added to make an even softer batter. There's the energy-filled version with walnuts, almonds, or hazelnuts, as well as the extra-tasty variation with chocolate shavings or a chocolate glaze.

Difficulty

RING CAKE
CIAMBELLA

Preparation time: 15 minutes + 30 minutes cooking time

4 Servings

1 1/4 cups (300 g) **unsalted butter,
 room temperature, plus more for pan**
4 **large eggs**
1 3/4 cups (400 g) **sugar**
Zest of 1 **lemon, grated**
2 1/4 lb. (1 kg) **all-purpose flour**
2 tsp. **baking powder**
4/5 cup (200 ml) **milk**

Method

Heat the oven to 400°F (200°C).

Butter a 10-inch (26 cm) ring mold.

With an electric mixer on medium, beat the eggs and the sugar in a bowl.

Add the butter and lemon zest to the egg mixture.

In a separate bowl, whisk together the flour and baking powder. Slowly add the flour mixture to the butter mixture. Add the milk. Mix until the batter is soft and smooth.

Bake for 30 minutes, or until golden brown. Let cool.

Difficulty

FRANGIPANE SOUR CHERRY CAKE

TORTA FRANGIPANE ALLE AMARENE

Preparation time: 35 minutes + 35 minutes cooking time

4 to 6 Servings

FOR THE FILLING

1/3 cup (40 g) **almonds**
1/3 cup (40 g) **all-purpose flour**
1/4 cup (50 g) **unsalted butter**
3 **egg yolks plus** 2 **egg whites**
1/4 tsp. (2 g) baking soda
1/4 cup plus 2 1/2 tsp. (60 g) **sugar**

FOR THE DOUGH

7 oz. (200 g) **puff pastry dough (see p. 26)**
1/4 cup (70 g) **sour-cherry jam**
1/4 cup (60 g) **sour cherries in syrup, drained**

FOR THE TOPPING

Almonds
Confectioners' sugar

Method

Heat the oven to 350°F (180°C).

Using a food processor or blender, pulse the almonds and flour together until they are finely ground.

With an electric mixer, beat the butter with the ground nut and flour mixture.

One at a time, add the egg yolks and continue to mix. Add the baking soda.

Beat the egg whites with the sugar and add to the batter.

Roll out the puff pastry dough to about 1/10 inch (3 mm) thick. Line an 8-inch (20 cm) round cake pan with the dough.

Spread the sour-cherry jam over the dough and sprinkle some drained sour cherries on top. Pour the filling into the pan to three-quarters full.

Arrange a few whole almonds on top.

Bake for about 35 minutes or until golden brown.

Let the cake cool completely before removing it from the pan. Dust the surface with confectioners' sugar.

Difficulty

CHOCOLATE ALMOND TORTE
TORTA CAPRESE

Preparation time: 30 minutes + 45 minutes cooking time

4 Servings

FOR THE DOUGH

1/3 cup (50 g) **blanched almonds**
1/2 cup plus 2 tbsp. (60 g)
   **confectioners' sugar, plus more for
   dusting**
2 1/2 oz. (75 g) **dark chocolate, chopped**
5 tbsp. (70 g) **unsalted butter, room
   temperature, plus more for pan**
1 **large egg, separated, plus 1 large
   egg yolk**
All-purpose flour, for pan

Method

Heat the oven to 325°F (160°C).

In a food processor, grind the almonds with a quarter of the sugar. Set aside.

Melt the chocolate in a heatproof bowl set over (not in) a pan of simmering water.

In a separate bowl, cream the butter and the remaining sugar until pale and fluffy. Add the egg yolks and continue beating.

Add the warm, melted chocolate to the egg yolk mixture, then add the ground almonds and stir.

In another bowl, beat the egg white and gently fold into the chocolate mixture.

Butter and flour an 8-inch (20 cm) cake pan (or line with parchment paper). Pour the batter into the pan, filling three-quarters full. Bake for 40 to 45 minutes, or until a cake tester inserted in the middle comes out clean.

Transfer the pan to a wire rack to cool. Remove the cake from pan and dust with confectioners' sugar.

Difficulty

SCHMARREN WITH CARAMELIZED APPLES AND ICE CREAM

SCHMARREN CON MELE CARAMELLATE E GELATO

Preparation time: 40 minutes

4 Servings

FOR THE ICE CREAM

2 cups (500 g) **sour cream**
3/4 cup (100 g) **confectioners' sugar**
2 tbsp. (15 g) **powdered milk**
3 tbsp. (50 g) lemon juice

FOR THE *SCHMARREN*

1 1/4 cups (300 g) **milk**
2 tbsp. (30 g) **unsalted butter**
1/4 cup (70 g) **ricotta cheese**
2 **large egg yolks plus** 3 **egg whites**
1 1/2 tbsp. (20 g) **vanilla sugar**
 (see recipe below)
3/4 cup (100 g) **all-purpose flour**
1/2 lb. (200 g) **apples**
5 1/2 tbsp. (70 g) **sugar**
1 tbsp. (15 g) **unsalted butter**
1 tbsp. (10 g) **golden raisins**
Salt

Method

For the ice cream: Combine all the ingredients in a bowl and mix well. Cool rapidly to 40°F (4°C) by putting the mixture in a container and immersing in a bowl of ice water. Refrigerate for 6 hours; then process in an ice cream maker, according to manufacturer's instructions, until thick. Transfer to an airtight container and place in the freezer until firm.

For the *Schmarren*: Heat the oven to 325°F (160°C).

In a saucepan, bring the milk to a boil with the butter. Transfer to a food processor, gradually adding the ricotta, egg yolks, vanilla sugar, and flour.

Blend the batter for 5 minutes (if necessary, strain through a fine-mesh sieve); refrigerate the batter.

Peel the apples and slice them thinly. Coat them with the sugar and sauté in the butter in a pan over medium heat for 4 minutes. Remove from the heat and add the raisins.

Beat the egg whites with a pinch of salt until stiff peaks form. Fold one-third into the batter, mixing well. Add the remaining two-thirds, folding them in carefully.

Arrange the apples and raisins evenly in a nonstick cake pan. Pour the batter over the top. Bake for 10 to 15 minutes, or until golden brown.

Serve warm, topped with ice cream.

For the vanilla sugar: Combine seeds from 1 vanilla bean (split lengthwise and seeds scraped) with 2 cups granulated sugar. Bury the vanilla pod in sugar and place the mixture in an airtight container. Seal and let sit for at least 1 week.

Difficulty

NEAPOLITAN BABÀ WITH PASTRY CREAM AND WILD STRAWBERRIES

BABÀ NAPOLETANO CON CREMA PASTICCIERA E FRAGOLINE DI BOSCO

Preparation time: 30 minutes + 8 minutes cooking time + 2 hours rising time

4 Servings

FOR THE BABÀ

3 1/3 cups (500 g) **all-purpose flour (or Italian type "0")**

2/3 cup (150 g) **unsalted butter, room temperature, plus more for mold**s

9 **large eggs**

1/4 cup (50 g) **sugar**

2 tsp. (10 g) **salt**

1 tbsp. (20 g) **active dry yeast**

FOR THE SYRUP

2 cups (500 g) **water**

1 1/4 cups (250 g) **sugar**

Zest of 1 **orange, grated**

Zest of 1 **lemon, grated**

1 **vanilla bean, sliced lengthwise, seeds scraped**

FOR PASTRY CREAM

Follow the recipe on page 16, but add the zests of 1 orange and 1 lemon to the milk in the first step. Follow remaining steps as written.

Wild strawberries, for serving.

Method

For the babà: Use an electric mixer or food processor to mix the flour, 1/2 cup (100 g) butter, 8 eggs, sugar, salt, and the yeast until ingredients form a dough.

Transfer the dough to a bowl. Knead in the remaining egg and butter by hand, adding a little at a time to form a smooth, elastic dough. Let rise for about 1 hour, or until doubled in volume.

Beat the dough again with the mixer or food processor. Use a pastry bag to pipe the dough into individual buttered molds. Let rise for another hour. Bake the babà in the oven at 400°F (200°C) for about 8 minutes.

For the syrup: Bring the water to a boil with the sugar, orange and lemon zests, and vanilla bean in a small saucepan. Let cool until lukewarm. Discard the vanilla bean.

To serve, soak the babà in the syrup. Arrange the babà on a serving plate, accompanied by the pastry cream and the wild strawberries.

Difficulty

FIG TARTLET WITH GOAT'S MILK ICE CREAM AND ALMOND BRITTLE
CROSTATINA AI FICHI E GELATO AL FIOR DI LATTE DI CAPRA E MANDORLE CROCCANTI

Preparation time: 1 hour 30 minutes + 6 hours freezing time for ice cream

4 Servings

FOR THE ICE CREAM
2 cups (500 g) **goat's milk**
3/4 cup (150 g) **sugar**
1 **vanilla bean, sliced lengthwise, seeds scraped**
2 tbsp. (30 g) **powdered milk**
1 **large egg yolk**
1/2 cup (100 g) **heavy cream**

FOR THE ALMOND BRITTLE
3/4 cup (100 g) **blanched almonds**
1/2 cup (100 g) **superfine sugar**
1 **lemon, halved**
Vegetable oil

FOR THE TARTLETS
All-purpose flour, for dusting
10 oz. **short pastry (see p. 22)**
3 tbsp. (40 g) **fig preserves**
4 oz. (120 g) **figs, sliced**

Method

For the ice cream: Heat the goat's milk, sugar, and vanilla bean in a saucepan over medium to 195°F (90°C) on a candy thermometer. Remove from the heat. Whisk together the powdered milk and egg yolk and add to milk mixture, whisking to combine. Whisk in the cream and cook, stirring, for 10 seconds.

Cool to 40°F (4°C) by putting the mixture in a container and immersing it in ice water.

Refrigerate for 6 hours, remove the vanilla bean, then process in an ice cream maker, according to the manufacturer's instructions, until thick. Transfer to a container and place in the freezer until firm.

For the almond brittle: Heat the oven to 350°F (175°C).

Coarsely chop the almonds. Spread on a baking sheet and toast in the oven until golden brown.

Put the sugar in a heavy saucepan over medium-low heat. Stir only until the sugar dissolves. Bring to a boil and cook, without stirring, until the sugar is an amber color. Remove from the heat.

Add a few drops of lemon juice and the toasted almonds to the caramelized sugar. Mix well. Pour the brittle onto a lightly oiled 18-inch (20 cm) nonstick work surface.

Use a lightly oiled lemon to spread the brittle to about 17 inches (43 cm) in diameter. Let cool undisturbed, then break into small pieces. (Brittle can be stored for up to 10 days.)

For the tartlets: Heat the oven to 350°F (180°C). On a lightly floured surface, roll out the short pastry to 1/3 inch (1 cm) thick. Cut into 4 rounds and line 4 dessert molds with a round. Spread fig preserves on the bottom of the pastry and arrange the fig slices on top. Bake for 15 minutes, or until golden brown.

Serve tartlets warm, topped with ice cream and almond brittle pieces.

Difficulty

RICOTTA PIE

CROSTATA DI RICOTTA

Preparation time: 40 minutes + 40 minutes cooking time

4 Servings

FOR THE DOUGH

7 tbsp. (100 g) **unsalted butter, room temperature**

1/2 cup (100 g) **sugar**

1 **large egg**

Zest of 1 **lemon, grated**

Salt

1 1/2 cups (200 g) **all-purpose flour, plus more for dusting**

1/2 tsp. (2 g) **baking powder**

Vegetable oil, for plastic wrap

FOR THE RICOTTA CREAM

2 **large eggs**

2/3 cup (130 g) **sugar**

Zest of 1 **lemon, grated**

3/4 cup (100 g) **almonds, roughly chopped**

2/3 cup (100 g) **pine nuts**

Method

For the dough: Use an electric mixer to cream the butter and sugar. Add the egg, lemon zest, and a pinch of salt.

Sift together the flour and the baking powder. Add the flour mixture to the butter mixture. Knead briefly until you have a smooth, uniform dough.

Form the dough into 2 disks and wrap them in lightly oiled plastic wrap. Refrigerate for at least 1 hour.

On a clean, lightly floured surface, roll out 1 disk of dough to 1/10 inch (3 mm) thick. Keep the other disk refrigerated.

Place the dough in a buttered and floured tart pan, lining the bottom and sides.

For the ricotta cream: Pass the ricotta through a sieve.

Whisk together the eggs and sugar in a large bowl. Add the lemon zest, followed by the ricotta, almonds, and pine nuts (set aside a few pine nuts for garnish).

Pour the ricotta cream into the crust.

Roll out the second disk of dough and cut it into strips. Arrange strips of dough on top of filling (in a lattice pattern, if desired).

Bake the pie for about 40 minutes, or until crust is golden brown.

Let it cool completely before removing from the pan.

Difficulty

SOFT-HEARTED CHOCOLATE CUPCAKES

TORTINI AL CIOCCOLATO CON CUORE MORBIDO

Preparation time: 20 minutes + 5 to 10 minutes cooking time

Makes 6 cupcakes

6 oz. (180 g) **dark chocolate, chopped**
3 tbsp. (40 g) **unsalted butter, plus more for pan**
5 **large egg whites plus** 2 **egg yolks**
1/4 cup (50 g) **sugar**
3/8 cup (50 g) **all-purpose flour, sifted, plus more for pan**

Method

In a heatproof bowl set over (not in) a pan of simmering water, melt the dark chocolate and butter.

Meanwhile, beat the egg whites in a bowl until frothy. Add the sugar and continue to beat until stiff peaks form.

Add the egg yolks to the egg whites and combine with the melted chocolate and butter.

Gently fold in the flour.

Butter and flour 6 cups of a muffin pan. Pour the batter into the cups, filling each three-quarters full.

Cover and refrigerate until well chilled, or freeze.

When ready to serve, bake in the oven at 400°F (200°C) for 5 to 6 minutes (8 to 10 minutes if the cupcakes were frozen).

Serve immediately, so that the centers (or hearts) of the cupcakes are still soft.

Difficulty

COOKIES AND CANDIES

CHAPTER THREE

PUMPKIN COOKIES
BISCOTTI ALLA ZUCCA

Preparation time: 45 minutes + 1 hour resting time + 20 minutes cooking time

4 Servings

7 oz. (200 g) **whole pumpkin**
7 tbsp. (100 g) **unsalted butter, room temperature, plus more for pan**
2/3 cup (150 g) **packed brown sugar**
1 **large egg, separated**
Cinnamon, to taste
Zest of 1/2 **lemon, grated**
Salt
2 1/2 cups (300 g) **all-purpose flour, plus more for dusting**
Sanding sugar, for decoration

Method

Wash the pumpkin and cut it into pieces, removing the seeds and fibers.

In a large pan of simmering water, steam the pumpkin for about 30 minutes or until very tender (alternatively, use a pressure cooker for 3 to 5 minutes).

Scoop out the flesh and discard the peel.

Place 3 1/2 ounces (100 grams), or about 1/2 cup, pumpkin in a large bowl. Add the butter, brown sugar, and the egg yolk and stir to combine.

Spice with cinnamon and lemon zest to taste, and season with a pinch of salt.

Add the flour and knead without overworking the dough. Form the dough into a ball and wrap it in plastic wrap. Refrigerate for 1 hour.

When ready to bake the cookies, heat the oven to 350°F (180°C).

On a clean, lightly floured work surface, roll the dough into a long log 1 1/2 inches (3 cm) in diameter.

Brush the log with egg white and sprinkle with sanding sugar.

Slice the log into disks about 1/2 inch (1 cm) thick.

Arrange the cookies on a baking sheet that is lightly buttered and floured (or lined with parchment).

Bake for about 20 minutes, or until golden brown.

CLASSIC AMARETTO COOKIES
AMARETTI CLASSICI

Preparation time: 20 minutes + 12 hours resting time + 17 to 18 minutes cooking time

4 to 6 Servings

1/3 cup (50 g) **almonds**
2/3 cup (130 g) **sugar**
1 **large egg white**

Method

In a food processor, pulse the almonds and sugar until finely ground.

Add half of the egg white (reserving the rest) to the almond mixture and pulse until well combined.

Cover the bowl with plastic wrap and let the mixture rest overnight.

When ready to bake the cookies, heat the oven to 325°F (170°C).

Knead the reserved egg white into the cookie dough, which should be soft but hold its shape. With wet hands, form the dough into about a dozen balls.

Arrange the balls on a parchment-lined baking sheet and press down lightly on each one.

Bake for 17 to 18 minutes, or until golden brown.

Difficulty

COCONUT COOKIES
BISCOTTI AL COCCO

Preparation time: 5 minutes + 10 minutes cooking time

4 Servings

1 1/2 cups (170 g) **coconut flour**
1/3 cup (40 g) **all-purpose flour**
1 cup (200 g) **granulated sugar**
2 **large eggs**
Salt
Confectioners' sugar (optional)
Unsweetened cocoa powder (optional)

Method

Heat the oven to 275°F (140°C).

On a clean work surface, mix together the flours and sugar. Form a well in the center, then add the eggs and a pinch of salt to the well. Mix together until you have a smooth dough.

Form the dough into balls, about 1/2 inch (1 cm) in diameter.

Arrange the balls on a parchment-lined baking pan, pressing down lightly on each one.

Bake for about 10 minutes, or until golden, and roll in either confectioners' sugar or cocoa.

Difficulty

LADY'S KISSES

BACI DI DAMA

Preparation time: 40 minutes + 30 minutes resting time + 15 minutes cooking time

4 Servings

3/4 cup (100 g) **roasted hazelnuts**
1/4 cup (25 g) **blanched almonds**
1/2 cup plus 2 tbsp. (125 g) **sugar**
1/2 cup (125 g) **unsalted butter, room temperature, plus more for baking sheet**
1 cup (125 g) **all-purpose flour, plus more for dusting**
3/8 cup (30 g) **unsweetened cocoa powder**
3 1/2 oz. (100 g) **dark chocolate**

Method

In a blender or food processor, pulse the hazelnuts and almonds with the sugar until finely ground.

In a bowl, combine the hazelnut mixture with the butter.

In another bowl, sift together the flour and cocoa, then incorporate into the butter mixture, stirring it as little as possible.

Wrap the mixture in plastic wrap and refrigerate for at least 30 minutes.

Heat the oven to 325°F (160°C).

On a clean, lightly floured work surface, roll out the chilled mixture to a thickness of about 3/8 inch (1 cm). Cut out disks with pastry rings 5/8 to 3/4 inch (1 1/2 to 2 cm) in diameter and shape into balls.

Arrange the balls on a lightly buttered, floured (or parchment-lined) baking sheet. Bake in the oven for about 15 minutes.

Let cool completely, then transfer from the baking sheet and invert them (rounded side down).

Meanwhile, melt the chocolate in a heatproof bowl set over (not in) a pan of simmering water, or in the microwave. Let it cool until it begins to crystallize.

Pour a little on each of half the batch of cookies. Place the flatter side of another cookie on top of each and allow the lady's kisses to set.

Difficulty

GLAZED HAZELNUT COOKIES

BISCOTTI GLASSATI ALLA NOCCIOLA

Preparation time: 30 minutes + 2 hours resting time + 10-12 minutes cooking time

4 to 6 Servings

FOR THE COOKIES

2/3 cup (150 g) **unsalted butter, room temperature**

1 cup plus 2 tsp. (125 g) **confectioners' sugar**

1 **large egg**

Zest of 1 **lemon, grated**

Vanilla extract

2 1/2 cups (300 g) **all-purpose flour, plus more for dusting**

3/4 tsp. (2 1/2g) **baking powder**

Salt

3/4 cup (100 g) **whole hazelnuts, toasted and ground into flour**

FOR THE GLAZE

1 **large egg white**

2/3 cup (120 g) **sugar**

3 3/4 tsp. (10 g) **cornstarch**

Method

With an electric mixer on medium-high speed, cream the butter with the confectioners' sugar.

Add the egg, lemon zest, and a dash of vanilla.

Sift together the flour, baking powder, a pinch of salt, and the hazelnut flour and combine with the butter mixture. Knead for a few minutes.

Form the dough into a ball, wrap in plastic wrap, and refrigerate for at least 1 hour.

When the dough is ready to bake, heat the oven to 350°F (180°C).

To prepare the glaze, beat the egg white with the sugar until the mixture is light and fluffy. Add the cornstarch and beat to combine.

On a clean, lightly floured work surface, roll out the dough to between 1/8 and 1/4 inch (4 mm) thick.

Place the dough on a parchment-lined surface. Spread the glaze over the dough and let sit for 1 hour.

Cut out the cookies in any shape you desire and arrange on a baking sheet. Bake for 10 to 12 minutes.

Difficulty

ALMOND BISCOTTI
CANTUCCINI

Preparation time: 20 minutes + 20 minutes cooking time

Makes about 1 lb. (500 g) of cookies

2 cups (250 g) all-purpose flour, plus
  more for dusting
1/2 tsp. (2 g) baking powder
Salt
7/8 cup (175 g) sugar
2 large eggs plus 2 large egg yolks
4 1/2 oz. (125 g) whole, unskinned
  almonds
Vanilla extract, to taste

Method

Heat the oven to 360°F (180°C). Sift together the flour, baking powder, and a pinch of salt in a large bowl. In a medium bowl, mix the sugar, eggs and egg yolk. Add the egg mixture to flour mixture and stir until the dough is well blended and smooth. Add almonds and vanilla, and stir to combine.

Divide the dough in half. On a clean, floured work surface, form the dough into logs about 12 inches (30 1/2 cm) long by 2 1/2 inches (6 cm) wide. Place the logs on a parchment-lined baking pan.

Bake in the oven for about 20 minutes, or until golden brown.

Remove the logs from the oven and immediately cut them with a serrated knife into 1/2-inch-wide diagonal slices. Place the slices, cut side down, on the same baking sheet and return to the oven for 10 minutes more, or until golden brown on both sides.

Difficulty

BASKET COOKIES
CANESTRELLI

Preparation time: 20 minutes + 1 hour resting time + 15 minutes cooking time

Makes about 1 lb. (500 g) of cookies

3/4 cup plus 1 tbsp. (185 g) **unsalted butter, room temperature**

3/4 cup (85 g) **confectioners' sugar, plus more for dusting**

1 **large egg yolk**

Zest of 1 **lemon, grated**

Vanilla extract

2 cups (250 g) **all-purpose flour, plus more for dusting**

Salt

Method

On a clean work surface, knead together the butter and confectioners' sugar.

Add the egg yolk, lemon zest, and a dash of vanilla and knead until combined.

Sift together the flour and the salt. Add to the dough and continue to knead until well combined.

Form the dough into a ball and wrap in plastic wrap. Refrigerate the dough for at least 1 hour.

When the dough is ready to bake, heat the oven to 325°F (170°C).

On a clean, lightly floured surface, roll out the dough to about 3/8 inch (1 cm) thick. Using a notched cookie cutter (or a daisy-shaped cutter), cut shapes from the dough, then cut a hole in the center of each (you can also find special canestrelli cookie cutters in Italian shops).

Arrange the cookies on a parchment-lined baking sheet.

Bake for about 15 minutes, or until golden.

Let the cookies cool. Sprinkle with confectioners' sugar.

A Crispy Spring

Canestrelli are exquisite, crispy cookies shaped like daisies, with a hole in the center and dusted with powdered sugar. They are typical of both Liguria and Piedmont, but in Piedmont hazelnut flour is added to the dough. The cookies are made to celebrate the arrival of spring, and in the past may have been presented during the Easter season in canestri (baskets) made of straw or wicker, thus giving rise to their name.

Difficulty

WHIPPED SHORTBREAD COOKIES

FROLLINI MONTATI

Preparation time: 15 minutes + 15 minutes resting time + 15 minutes cooking time

4 to 6 Servings

3/4 cup (165 g) **unsalted butter, room temperature**

1 cup plus 2 tbsp. (135 g) **confectioners' sugar**

2 **large eggs**

Zest of 1 **lemon, grated**

Vanilla extract

1/2 tsp. (2 g) **salt**

2 3/4 cups (335 g) **all-purpose flour, sifted**

Method

Using a mixer with a whisk attachment, beat the butter and the confectioners' sugar. Add the eggs, lemon zest, a dash of vanilla, and the salt; mix well. Add the flour, stirring briefly.

Use a pastry bag with a basketweave decorating tip to immediately pipe the cookies onto parchment-lined baking sheets. Refrigerate for at least 15 minutes.

Heat the oven to 350°F (180°C). Bake the cookies for 13 to 15 minutes, or until golden brown.

Difficulty

Whipped Short Pastry Dough

Whipped short pastry dough is a classic confectionary staple and is used to make shortbread cookies shaped with a pastry bag or cookie press, since the dough is much softer and creamier than that of the traditional recipe. These cookies are easy and quick to make, but are impressive for their softness and flavor.

BULL'S-EYES

OCCHI DI BUE

Preparation time: 40 minutes + 13 to 15 minutes cooking time + 45 minutes resting time

Makes 1 dozen cookies

All-purpose flour, for dusting
14 oz. (400 g) **short pastry dough (see p. 22)**
5 oz. (150 g) **jam (choose your favorite flavor)**
Confectioners' sugar, for dusting

Method

Heat the oven to 350°F (180°C).

On a clean, lightly floured surface, roll out the short pastry dough between 1/8 and 1/4 inch (4–5 mm) thick. Using a cookie cutter of your choice, cut out twenty-four 2-inch (5 cm) disks.

Divide the disks between two parchment-lined baking sheets. Using a 1 1/2-inch (4 cm) cookie cutter, cut out the centers of the disks on the first baking sheet to create rings.

Bake the cookies for 12 to 13 minutes, or until golden brown. Remove the baking sheet with the rings a couple of minutes before the other sheet.

Let the rings and disks cool completely, about 45 minutes.

Turn over the disks and spread the borders with a little jam, then place the rings on top, pressing to adhere. Dust the bull's-eyes with confectioners' sugar.

Heat the jam and then fill the center of each bull's-eye.

From Egg to Cookie

This traditional jam-filled short-pastry-dough sweet, which makes an excellent snack with a good cup of tea, gets its name from the similarity of its appearance to an Italian egg recipe called bull's-eye eggs (pan-fried eggs, where the round white surrounds the yolk "pupil"). Bull's-eye cookies are usually prepared by layering two round cookies, one without a center, filled with apricot jam (the yellow color of which resembles that of the yolk in the egg dish). But you can give your imagination free rein in choosing the flavor of jam (strawberry and plum are delicious), or opt for chocolate, hazelnut, or coffee cream spread instead. The shapes can also vary, whether inspired by nature, such as flowers, hearts, or stars, or strictly geometric.

Difficulty

CORNMEAL COOKIES
PASTE DI MELIGA

Preparation time: 15 minutes + 1 hour resting time + 15 minutes cooking time

4 to 6 Servings

1 cup (225 g) **unsalted butter, room temperature**
1/2 cup plus 1 tbsp. (115 g) **sugar**
2 rounded tsp. (15 g) **honey**
1 **l arge egg**
Zest of 1 **lemon, grated**
Vanilla extract
1/2 tsp. (2 g) **salt**
2 cups (260 g) **all-purpose flour, plus more for dusting**
1/2 cup plus 4 1/2 tsp. (75 g) **finely ground cornmeal**

Method

With an electric mixer on medium high, cream the butter with the sugar and honey. Add the egg, lemon zest, a dash of vanilla, and the salt; mix well.

Sift together the flour and the cornmeal. Add to the dough, mixing until combined.

Form the dough into a ball and wrap it in plastic wrap. Refrigerate for about 1 hour.

When the dough is ready to bake, heat the oven to 350°F (180°C).

On a clean, lightly floured surface, roll out the dough to about 1/4 inch (6 mm) thick.

Using a cookie cutter, cut out disks about 2 inches in diameter. Arrange them on parchment-lined baking sheets.

Bake for about 15 minutes, or until golden brown.

Yellow Goodness from Cuneo

Cornmeal cookies are typical of the town of Cuneo, in Piedmont. The word meliga is local dialect for "maize." According to tradition, they are of ancient origin and were invented during a year when the price of wheat flour rose prohibitively high. Bakers decided to add a little finely ground corn flour to the dough, an ingredient that not only gave the cookies a distinctive taste but also a very crumbly texture. Traditionally, meliga shortbread cookies are eaten with zabaglione cream, along with a small glass of Barolo Chinato.

Difficulty

LADYFINGERS

SAVOIARDI

Preparation time: 20 minutes + 10 to 15 minutes cooking time

Makes about 30 ladyfingers

1 cup (125 g) **all-purpose flour**
5 1/2 tsp. (15 g) **cornstarch**
3 **large eggs plus 1 large egg yolk**
2/3 cup plus 1 1/2 tsp. (140 g) **sugar**
Vanilla extract
1 1/2 tsp. (10 g) **honey, heated in a small pan, stirring constantly**
Zest of 1/4 **lemon, grated**
Confectioners' sugar, for dusting

Method

Heat the oven to 400°F (200°C).

Sift together the flour and the cornstarch and set aside. In a medium bowl, beat the eggs and egg yolk with the sugar, a dash of vanilla, and the warm honey.

Add the lemon zest, then stir in the flour mixture.

Using a pastry bag with a large plain tip, pipe the ladyfingers onto baking sheets lined with parchment paper.

Dust with confectioners' sugar and bake for 10 to15 minutes, until golden brown.

The History of Ladyfingers

Ladyfingers, light cookies with a rounded, oblong shape, date to the end of the fifteenth century, when they were created by the chefs of the dukes of Savoy to celebrate the visit of the king of France. Despite their Piedmontese origin, ladyfingers are found in the artisan confectionary traditions of all the regions of Italy that were once under Savoy influence. This explains their presence in Sardinia, where they are also called pistoccus de caffè, which refers to the fact that they are delicious dunked in coffee. Thanks to their crisp, spongy texture, which makes them perfect for dipping, they are also used in famous creamy dessert recipes, like tiramisù and zuppa inglese.

Difficulty

FAN COOKIES
VENTAGLI

Preparation time: 20 minutes + 15 minutes cooking time

4 to 6 Servings

Superfine sugar
11 oz. (300 g) **puff pastry dough (see p. 26)**

Method

Heat the oven to 450°F (230°C)

On a clean surface lightly sprinkled with superfine sugar, roll out the puff pastry dough in a rectangle between 1/8 and 1/16 inch (2 mm) thick. Sprinkle the rectangle with more superfine sugar, then roll up the dough from both ends to form two scrolls that meet in the middle.

Press the two rolls together so that they meet perfectly. Lightly press one against the other, then cut into 3/4-inch (2 cm) slices.

Press the slices in the sugar and arrange in neat, well-spaced rows on very clean baking sheets (unbuttered).

Bake for about 15 minutes, turning them over halfway through, until they are golden.

Fan Cookies: Simple and Striking

With their tasty sugar coating and simple puff pastry ingredients, easy-to-make fan cookies are loved by all. Make them even more delicious with the addition of chocolate chips, coconut shavings, raisins, or even a chocolate glaze. Even when prepared at home, these fragrant sweets will be equal to the ones found at cafés and pastry shops. Fan cookies, so named for their distinctive shape, are perfect for any time of day: breakfast, snack time, or after a meal. For savory variations perfect for serving with aperitifs, substitute grated Parmigiano-Reggiano for the sugar, grating the cheese over the puff pastry dough, or spread the dough with tomato sauce and olives or sun-dried tomatoes and rosemary.

Difficulty

TURIN CHOCOLATES

CREMINO TORINO

Preparation time: 1 hour and 30 minutes + 12 hours resting time

Makes about 30 chocolates

DARK CHOCOLATE MIXTURE

3/4 cup (100 g) **whole hazelnuts, toasted**
1/2 cup (100 g) **sugar**
3 1/2 oz. (100 g) **dark chocolate**
Lemon juice

MILK CHOCOLATE MIXTURE

3/4 cup (100 g) **whole hazelnuts, toasted**
3/4 cup plus 4 tsp. (100 g) **confectioners' sugar**
5 oz. (150 g) **milk chocolate**

Method

For the dark chocolate mixture: Heat the oven to 200°F (100°C). Place the toasted hazelnuts on a baking sheet and keep warm in the oven.

In a saucepan (preferably of copper) over medium heat, cook the sugar and a few drops of lemon juice until the sugar begins to caramelize and it is golden brown.

Add the warmed hazelnuts, coating them with the mixture.

Pour the nuts onto a marble surface (or other nonstick surface) coated with oil and let cool completely.

Break up the resulting brittle into pieces and pulse in a food processor until it becomes an oily mass.

In a heatproof bowl over (not in) a pan of simmering water (or in the microwave), melt the dark chocolate and add it to the hazelnut mixture, stirring to combine.

Pour half of the dark chocolate mixture into a container lined with parchment and let cool.

In the meantime, prepare **the milk chocolate mixture:** In a food processor, pulse the hazelnuts and confectioners' sugar together until they become an oily mass.

In a heatproof bowl set over (not in) a pan of simmering water (or in a microwave), melt the milk chocolate and add it to the hazelnut mixture, stirring to combine.

Pour the milk chocolate mixture over half the dark chocolate mixture in the container and let cool. As soon as the milk chocolate mixture has hardened, cover it with the other half of the dark mixture.

Let set at least overnight in a cool place (preferably not in the refrigerator). Then cut into small squares and serve.

Difficulty

106

CUNEO RUM MERINGUE COOKIES
CUNEESI AL RUM

Preparation time: 2 hours and 40 minutes + 20 minutes cooking time

Makes about 25 cookies

FOR THE MERINGUES

1 **egg white**
1/4 cup plus 2 1/2 tsp. (60 g) **sugar**
1 1/2 tsp. (3 g) **sweetened cocoa powder**

FOR THE FILLING

5 oz. (150 g) **dark chocolate, chopped**
3 1/2 tbsp. (50 g) **heavy cream**
3 tbsp. plus 1 tsp. (50 ml) **corn syrup**
1/3 oz. (10 g) **hazelnut paste**
1/2 cup plus 1 1/4 tsp. (125 ml) **rum**
Vanilla extract
1 3/4 oz. (50 g) **pastry cream (see p. 16)**

FOR THE GLAZE

5 oz. (150 g) **dark chocolate**

Method

Heat the oven to 375°F (190°C).

For meringues: In a clean bowl, beat egg white until frothy. Add 1 1/2 tablespoons of sugar and continue to beat mixture until stiff, glossy peaks form.

Mix remaining sugar with cocoa and gently fold into egg mixture.

Use a pastry bag with a smooth 3/8-inch (1 cm) tip to pipe meringues onto a parchment-lined baking sheet.

Bake meringues for about 20 minutes, until dried and crisp but not browned.

Just after baking, gently remove meringues from parchment. With your thumb, lightly press bottom of each meringue, creating a shallow indentation.

For filling: Place chocolate in a medium heatproof bowl.

In a saucepan over medium-high heat, bring cream and corn syrup to a gentle simmer. Pour cream mixture over chocolate. Stir until it becomes a velvety cream.

Add hazelnut paste, rum, and a dash of vanilla and mix well. Stir in the pastry cream.

Let filling firm; then, with meringues in pairs, spoon filling into indentations of each meringue. Press together to make one "sandwich" cookie.

For glaze: Melt dark chocolate in a heatproof bowl over (not in) a pan of simmering water (or a bain-marie) until it reaches between 110°F and 120°F (45°C–50°C) on a candy thermometer.

Pour half of chocolate onto a marble surface and, using a spatula to spread it, cool to between 78°F and 81°F (26°C–27°C). Add it to the remaining hot glaze. When it reaches 90°F (32°C), it is ready to use.

Carefully dip meringues in the chocolate glaze to coat. Let glazed cookies set on a wire rack.

Difficulty

RASPBERRY GUMMY CANDIES

GELATINE AL LAMPONE

Preparation time: 15 minutes + 10 minutes cooking time + 1 hour resting time

Makes about 100 candies

2 1/2 cups (300 g) **raspberries**
2 cups (400 g) **granulated sugar**
3/4 oz. (20 g) **powdered pectin**
1/2 cup plus 6 1/2 tsp. (150 ml) **water**
3/4 cup (175 ml) **corn syrup**
1 tbsp. (5 g) **lemon juice**
Superfine sugar

Method

In a blender or food processer, blend the raspberries. Pass the raspberry mixture through a sieve to remove the seeds, then weigh out about 8 ounces (230 g) of raspberry pulp.

In a saucepan over medium-high heat, combine 1/4 cup (50 g) granulated sugar with the pectin, add the raspberry pulp and the water, and bring to a boil.

Add the remaining granulated sugar and the corn syrup, then heat to 220°F (106°C) on a candy thermometer.

Add the lemon juice and stir to combine.

Immediately pour the mixture into silicone candy molds or into a square or rectangular mold lined with parchment. Let cool.

If you used a parchment-lined pan, cut the candies into cubes or small shapes with a knife once the mixture has cooled.

Bring a pan of water to a boil.

Remove the gummy candies from the molds, place in a sieve, and pass briefly over the steam from the pan of boiling water. Roll the candies in superfine sugar.

Let sit for about 1 hour before serving (or packaging in an airtight container).

Candies That Melt in Your Mouth

These fruity candies with a wonderful gummy texture, covered with superfine sugar, can be made with the juice of any fresh seasonal fruit: strawberries, peaches, pineapple, berries, kiwi, mandarin oranges, and so on. They are truly delicious and should be kept in the refrigerator in an airtight glass container.

'fficulty

FAVORITES (CHOCOLATE-COVERED CHERRIES)
PREFERITI

Preparation time: 1 hour + 24 hours resting time

4 Servings

12 **brandied cherries**
9 oz. (250 g) **dark chocolate**
Cornstarch

FOR THE SUGAR FONDANT

1 cup (200 g) **sugar**
2 tbsp. (30 ml) **corn syrup**
2 tbsp. plus 2 tsp. (40 ml) **water**

Difficulty

Method

Drain the cherries and gently dry them.

For the sugar fondant: Heat the sugar, corn syrup, and water in a saucepan (preferably copper). Heat the mixture to 240°F (115°C) on a candy thermometer. Brush the sides of the saucepan with a damp pastry brush to keep crystals from forming.

Slowly pour the sugar mixture onto a slightly damp marble (or other nonstick) work surface, letting it cool for about 4 minutes.

Using a wooden spatula, begin to work the mixture, gathering the sugar from the edges toward the center. After working the sugar mixture for a few minutes, it will begin to turn uniformly white.

Melt the fondant in a heatproof bowl set over (not in) a pan of simmering water. Gently dip the cherries into the fondant to glaze them.

Fill a container with cornstarch. Arrange the cherries on the cornstarch, to prevent their bases from flattening. Let the glazed cherries harden.

Temper the dark chocolate: In a heatproof bowl set over (not in) a pan of simmering water (or a bain-marie), melt the chocolate until it reaches between 110°F and 120°F (45°C–50°C) on a candy thermometer.

Pour about half of the chocolate onto a marble surface and, using a spatula to spread it around, cool to between 78°F and 81°F (26°C–27°C). Add it to the remaining hot glaze. When it reaches 90°F (32°C), it is ready to use.

Coat the fondant-covered cherries with the tempered chocolate.

Let rest for 24 hours before serving, so the alcohol has time to dissolve the sugar inside the chocolate coating.

RICH SHORTBREAD COOKIES

FROLLINI ALL'UOVO

Preparation time: 15 minutes + 1 hour chilling time + 18 minutes cooking time

Makes about 1 1/2 lbs. (650 g) of cookies

5 large eggs, for boiling
1 vanilla bean
2 1/2 cups (300 g) all-purpose flour,
  plus more for dusting
3/4 cup (100 g) cornstarch
Salt
1 1/4 cups (250 g) unsalted butter,
  room temperature
1 1/4 cups (125 g) confectioners' sugar
Vegetable oil, for plastic wrap

Method

For hard-cooked egg yolks: Cover the eggs with water in a saucepan and bring to a boil over high heat. Reduce the heat to low and simmer for 8 to 10 minutes.

Drain the eggs and immediately plunge them in cold water to stop the cooking process and make them easier to peel. Peel the eggs, then separate the yolks from the whites (which are not used in this recipe).

Make the cookies: Slice the vanilla bean lengthwise and scrape out the seeds from one half (reserve other half bean for another use).

Whisk the vanilla seeds, flour, cornstarch, and a pinch of salt in a bowl.

Cream the butter and confectioners' sugar.

Run the egg yolks through a sieve. Mix them into the butter mixture until completely incorporated. Add the flour mixture. Knead the mixture until it is a smooth dough. Wrap the dough in lightly oiled plastic wrap and refrigerate for at least 1 hour.

Heat the oven to 350°F (170°C).

On a clean, lightly floured work surface, roll out the dough to 1/6 inch (4 mm) thick. With a cookie cutter, cut into desired shapes.

Arrange the shortbread cookies on a parchment-lined baking sheet and bake for about 18 minutes, or until golden brown.

Difficulty

ASSORTED TRUFFLES

TARTUFI DOLCI ASSORTITI

Preparation time: 45 minutes + 4 hours cooling time

4 Servings

FOR DARK CHOCOLATE TRUFFLES

2 1/4 oz. (65 g) **dark chocolate, chopped**

1/8 cup (12 g) **unsweetened cocoa powder, plus more for dusting**

3/8 cup (50 g) **toasted hazelnuts, chopped**

1 cup (100 g) **confectioners' sugar**

4 tsp. (20 ml) **light extra-virgin olive oil**

FOR WHITE CHOCOLATE TRUFFLES

2 oz. (60 g) **white chocolate, chopped**

4 1/2 tbsp. (60 g) **hazelnut paste**

3 tbsp. (25 g) **toasted hazelnuts, chopped**

2 tsp. (2 g) **unsweetened cocoa powder**

5/8 cup (65 g) **confectioners' sugar, plus more for dusting**

FOR PISTACHIO TRUFFLES

7 oz. (200 g) **white chocolate, chopped**

4 tsp. (25 g) **pistachio paste**

3 1/2 tbsp. (30 g) **pistachios, chopped, plus 3/8 cup (50 g) chopped for topping**

Confectioners' sugar, for work surface

Difficulty

Method

For dark chocolate truffles: Melt the chocolate in a heatproof bowl set over (not in) a pan of simmering water. Mix in remaining ingredients, adding oil as needed, until smooth. Let the chocolate mixture cool for at least 4 hours at room temperature.

On a work surface dusted with cocoa, roll the cooled chocolate into lengths, then cut into 1-inch (2 1/2 cm) pieces. Form the pieces into balls (they need not be uniform) and roll them in the cocoa.

For white chocolate truffles: Melt the chocolate as directed above, then mix in the hazelnut paste, hazelnuts, and cocoa until smooth. Cool as directed above. On a work surface dusted with confectioners' sugar, roll the cooled chocolate into lengths, cut into 1-inch (2 1/2 cm) pieces and form into balls. Dust with confectioners' sugar.

For pistachio truffles: Melt 3 1/2 ounces of the chocolate as directed above, then stir in pistachio paste and 3 1/2 tablespoons (30 g) chopped pistachios until smooth. Cool as directed above. On a work surface dusted with confectioners' sugar, roll cooled chocolate into lengths, cut into 1-inch (2 1/2 cm) pieces and form into balls. Melt the remaining chocolate, cool slightly and dip truffles to coat. Immediately roll the truffles in 3/8 cup (50 g) chopped pistachios.

CHOCOLATE DESSERT "SALAMI"

SALAME AL CIOCCOLATO

Preparation time: 3 hours

Makes 1 salami

2 oz. (50 g) **plain biscotti, coarsely crushed**

1 tbsp. (10 g) **toasted hazelnuts**

1 tbsp. (10 g) **pistachios**

1 tbsp. (10 g) **pine nuts**

1 tbsp. (10 g) **sweet almonds**

4 oz. (120 g) **chocolate with hazelnuts, chopped**

5 tsp. (25 g) **unsalted butter, room temperature**

Confectioners' sugar, for dusting

Method

In a bowl, combine the biscotti, toasted hazelnuts, pistachios, pine nuts, and sweet almonds.

Melt the chocolate with the hazelnuts and butter in a bowl set over (not in) a pan of simmering water. Let it cool slightly, then pour over the biscotti-and-nut mixture.

Let the mixture harden just enough so that you can still mix and shape it.

On a work surface dusted with confectioners' sugar, form the chocolate mixture into a sausage shape.

Sprinkle more confectioners' sugar over the chocolate salami. Wrap it in waxed paper, tying it with kitchen string to resemble a meat salami, if desired.

Difficulty

CHOCOLATE HAZELNUT BISCOTTI

BISCOTTINI CROCCANTI AL CACAO E NOCCIOLE

Preparation time: 20 minutes + 10 to 12 minutes cooking time

4 Servings

1 cup (125 g) **confectioners' sugar**
1/4 cup (25 g) **unsweetened cocoa
powder**
2 tbsp. (15 g) **cornstarch**
1 tsp. (5 g) **baking powder**
1 **large egg white**
1/2 tsp. (3 ml) **vanilla extract**
1/2 cup (75 g) **chopped toasted
hazelnuts**
Unsalted butter and all-purpose flour,
for pans

Method

Heat the oven to 340°F (170°C).

Sift together the confectioners' sugar, cocoa, cornstarch, and baking powder in a bowl.

Stir in the egg white and vanilla until smooth. Add the hazelnuts and stir.

On a lightly floured work surface, form the mixture into a log about 1 1/4 inches (3 cm) in diameter. Cut into slices 3/8 inch (1 cm) thick.

Butter and flour a baking sheet, or line with parchment. Arrange the biscotti on baking sheet and bake for 10 to 12 minutes.

Let cool completely before removing from the pan.

Difficulty

PASTRIES

CHAPTER FOUR

CREAM PUFFS
BIGNÈ ALLA CREMA

Preparation time: 25 minutes + 20 minutes cooking time

4 Servings

Cream puff pastry dough (see p. 24)

FOR THE CREAM FILLING

2 cups (500 ml) **milk**

1 **vanilla bean, split lengthwise, seeds scraped**

4 **large egg yolks**

3/4 cup (150 g) **sugar**

1/8 cup (20 g) **all-purpose flour**

2 1/2 tbsp. (20 g) **cornstarch**

Method

Prepare and bake the cream puff pastry dough (follow the recipe on p. 24).

Meanwhile, prepare the filling: Bring the milk to a boil in a saucepan with half the vanilla bean (reserve remaining half bean for another use).

Whisk the egg yolks with sugar in a bowl. In another bowl, sift together the flour and cornstarch; whisk into the egg yolk mixture.

Pour a quarter of the boiling milk into the egg yolk mixture and stir until smooth. Add this mixture to the remaining milk over medium heat, whisking constantly and returning it to a boil, until thick.

Pour the cooked cream filling into a bowl and immerse the bowl in ice water to cool it quickly. Cut off the top of each pastry puff and use a pastry bag to fill with cream.

Difficulty

PUMPKIN AND POPPY PUFFS
SFOGLIATINE ALLA ZUCCA E PAPAVERO

Preparation time: 40 minutes + 20 minutes cooking time

4 Servings

7 oz. (200 g) **puff pastry dough**
  (see p. 26)

FOR THE CREAM FILLING
12 oz. (350 g) **pumpkin**
1/8 cup (20 g) **poppy seeds**
1 tbsp. plus 1 tsp. (20 g) **unsalted butter**
1 tsp. (10 g) **honey**
1 1/2 tbsp. (20 g) **raw sugar**
Salt

FOR FINISHING
1 **large egg, lightly beaten**

Method

Wash and peel the pumpkin, removing seeds and fibers. Cut the pumpkin into 1-inch (2 cm) pieces.

Coarsely grind the poppy seeds (you can use a coffee grinder).

Melt the butter in a large pan. Add the ground poppy seeds and cook over low heat for 2 to 3 minutes.

Add the pumpkin, honey, sugar, and a pinch of salt and cook for about 10-15 minutes, or until pumpkin is tender. Let cool.

Meanwhile, heat the oven to 400°F (200°C).

Roll out the puff pastry dough to 2 inches (5 mm) thick.

With cookie cutters, cut disks about 4 inches (10 cm) in diameter and roll them into 1 1/2-inch (2-3 mm) thick ovals.

Brush the edges of the dough with some of the beaten egg. Place the filling in the center of the dough and fold to close.

Arrange the puff pastry on a parchment-lined baking sheet, then brush the surface with the remaining egg.

Bake for about 20 minutes.

Difficulty

CHANTILLY CREAM PUFFS
BIGNÈ CHANTILLY

Preparation time: 15 minutes

4 Servings

16 pastry puffs (sprinkled with sugar
    before baked) (use one-third cream
    puff pastry dough recipe on p. 24)
10 1/2 oz. (300 g) pastry cream
    (see p. 16)
1 3/4 cups (200 g) sweetened whipped
    cream
Confectioners' sugar

Method

Cut the tops from the pastry puffs and set them aside.

Use a pastry bag to fill the puffs, almost to the top, with pastry cream.

Use another pastry bag fitted with a star tip to add a dollop of whipped cream.

Cover the cream puffs with the reserved pastry tops.

Refrigerate in an airtight container until ready to serve.

Before serving, dust the cream puffs with confectioners' sugar.

Chantilly Cream

In Italy, Chantilly cream almost always means a combination of pastry cream and whipped cream, as in this recipe. Historically, however, crème chantilly is simply the French name for sweetened, scented (often with vanilla) whipped cream. In the sixteenth century, whipped cream was already known and poetically called milk snow. Nevertheless, its invention is traditionally dated to the seventeenth century and attributed to François Vatel, majordomo of Chantilly Castle, a splendid estate in the city of the same name in northern France (where one also finds the Musée Condé, which houses an important collection of paintings, including Italian works, and old manuscripts).

Difficulty

PUFF PASTRY CANNOLI WITH ZABAGLIONE

CANNOLI DI SFOGLIA ALLO ZABAGLIONE

Preparation time: 30 minutes + 15 to 20 minutes cooking time

4 to 6 Servings

12 oz. (350 g) **puff pastry dough**
 (see p. 26)
Superfine sugar, for dusting

FOR THE ZABAGLIONE CREAM
2/3 cup (160 ml) **Marsala wine**
4 **large egg yolks**
1/3 cup + 1 tbsp. (80 g) **sugar**
1 tbsp. (8 g) **all-purpose flour**
1 tbsp. (8 g) **cornstarch**

1/4 cup (25 g) **whole hazelnuts, chopped**

Method

For the zabaglione cream: Heat the Marsala in a saucepan.

Meanwhile, beat the egg yolks and sugar in a copper or stainless-steel bowl.

Sift together the flour and cornstarch, then add to the egg mixture and mix well.

Pour a little of the boiling wine onto the eggs to temper them, then add the remaining Marsala and mix well. Return the mixture to the saucepan and bring to a boil, whisking constantly until it is as thick as custard. Transfer the zabaglione to a heatproof container and let cool.

Heat the oven to at 400°F (200°C).

On a clean, lightly floured surface, roll out the puff pastry dough to between 1/8 and 1/16 inch (2 mm) thick. Cut the dough into strips just over 1/2 inch (1 1/2 cm) wide and just under 6 inches long (15 cm).

Wrap the strips around specially designed metal cannoli forms, so each coil of dough slightly overlaps the one before it.

Place the cannoli in the superfine sugar and press lightly to coat the dough; only coat one side. Arrange the cannoli on a baking tray, with the sugar-coated side facing up.

Bake for 15 to 20 minutes, until the dough is cooked and the sugar caramelized.

Let cool, then gently detach the shells from the metal forms. Use a pastry bag to fill the cannoli with zabaglione. Sprinkle the openings of the cannoli with chopped hazelnuts.

Difficulty

SICILIAN CANNOLI
CANNOLI SICILIANI

Preparation time: 30 minutes + 1 to 1 1/2 hours resting time + 2 minutes cooking time

4 Servings

FOR THE PASTRY

3/4 cup plus 1 tbsp. (100 g) **all-purpose flour**

2 tbsp. (10 g) **unsweetened cocoa powder**

2 tsp. (10 g) **unsalted butter, room temperature**

1 **large egg**

3 1/2 tsp. (15 g) **sugar**

Salt

1 tbsp. (15 ml) **Marsala wine or rum**

FOR THE FILLING

8 3/4 oz. (250 g) **fresh ricotta, preferably made from sheep's milk**

1/2 cup (100 g) **sugar**

1 oz. (25 g) **candied fruit, roughly chopped**

1 oz. (25 g) **chocolate chips, or semisweet chocolate roughly chopped**

1 oz. (25 g) **pistachios, roughly chopped**

Vegetable oil, for frying

Confectioners' sugar, for dusting

Method

For the pastry: Combine the flour, cocoa, butter, egg, sugar, and a pinch of salt in a bowl.

Turn the mixture out onto a clean work surface, add the Marsala, and knead until the dough is smooth. Let it rest for 30 minutes.

In the meantime, prepare the filling. Run the ricotta through a sieve and combine it with the sugar, fruit, chocolate, and pistachios. Cover in plastic wrap and refrigerate until chilled, 30 to 60 minutes.

Roll out the dough to 1/8 inch (2 mm) thick and cut it into 4-inch (10-cm) squares. Wrap the squares diagonally around a special cannoli form (or stainless-steel dowels cut into 4-inch lengths).

Heat the oil in a pan until shimmering. Place the cannoli form with dough into the hot oil and fry until golden, 1 to 2 minutes. Remove from the oil, drain on paper towels, and let cool. Once the shells have cooled, remove them from the cannoli form.

Use a pastry bag to fill the cannoli with the ricotta filling, then dust with confectioners' sugar. Serve immediately (the moist filling soon makes the dough lose its crispness).

Difficulty

CHOCOLATE PROFITEROLES
PROFITEROLES AL CIOCCOLATO

Preparation time: 1 hour 30 minutes

4 Servings

Cream puff pastry dough (see p. 24)
Chocolate ganache (see p. 18)
8 oz. (230 g)   **pastry cream (see p. 16)**

Method

Prepare and bake the cream puff pastry dough (follow recipe on p. 24).

Prepare the chocolate ganache (follow the recipe on p. 18). Keep in mind that ganache must be refrigerated (in order to thicken) for 4 hours before using.

Prepare the pastry cream (follow the recipe on p. 16).

Use a pastry bag with a small plain tip to fill puffs with pastry cream. Refrigerate cream puffs in an airtight container until ready to serve.

Drizzle the cream puffs with chocolate ganache before serving.

Difficulty

FILLED CROISSANTS
SFOGLIATELLE RICCE

Preparation time: 1 hour + 2 hours resting time + 25 minutes cooking time

4 to 6 Servings

FOR THE PASTRY

2 1/3 cups plus 1 tbsp. (300 g) **all-purpose flour**

1/4 cup plus 2 tsp. (60 g) **lard, room temperature**

2 tbsp. plus 1 1/4 tsp. (30 g) **sugar**

1/2 tsp. (3 g) **salt**

1/2 cup (100 ml) **water**

FOR THE FILLING

1/2 tsp. (2 g) **salt**

1/2 cup (100 ml) **water**

8 1/2 tsp. (30 g) **semolina**

1/2 cup (100 g) **ricotta**

1/4 cup plus 2 1/2 tsp. (60 g) **sugar**

3/4 oz. (20 g) **candied orange peel, minced**

1 **large egg**

Zest of 1 **lemon, grated**

Ground cinnamon

1 **vanilla bean, split lengthwise, seeds scraped**

1/4 cup (60 g) **lard, room temperature**

Confectioners' sugar, for garnish

Difficulty

Method

For the pastry: Knead the flour together with the lard, sugar, and salt, gradually adding the water. When the dough becomes smooth and elastic, cover it in plastic wrap and refrigerate for 1 hour.

For the filling: Add the salt to the water in a small pot and bring to a boil. Sprinkle the semolina into the boiling water and cook for 3 to 4 minutes. Let cool.

Run the ricotta through a sieve and mix it with the sugar, candied orange peel, and egg. Add the lemon zest, a pinch of cinnamon, and the vanilla bean and stir to combine.

Using your hands, stretch and shape the dough into a rectangle, making it as thin as possible.

Spread the dough with a layer of softened lard and roll it up to form a log about 4 inches (10 cm) in diameter. Spread it with lard and refrigerate it for 1 hour.

When the dough is ready to be baked, heat the oven to 425°F (220°C).

Put the dough on a clean work surface and stretch the log with your hands.

Cut the log into slices about 1/2 inch thick, flatten them, and push up the center from the underside of each to form a kind of cone.

Fill the cones with the ricotta mixture, fold over and arrange them on parchment-lined baking sheets. Bake for about 25 minutes.

Remove from the oven and sprinkle with confectioners' sugar.

APPLE STRUDEL
STRUDEL DI MELE

Preparation time: 1 hour + 30 minutes resting time + 20 minutes cooking time

4 Servings

FOR THE DOUGH

2 cups (250 g) **all-purpose flour, plus more for dusting**

2/3 cup (150 ml) **water**

1 tbsp. plus 1 tsp. (20 ml) **extra-virgin olive oil, plus more for plastic wrap**

Salt

FOR THE FILLING

1 3/4 lbs. (800 g) **tart apples, such as Granny Smith**

3 1/2 oz. (100 g) **raisins, or** about 2/3 cup packed

1/2 stick (60 g) **unsalted butter, room temperature**

3 1/2 oz. (100 g) **pine nuts, or** about 2/3 cup

Ground cinnamon

2–3 1/2 oz. (60–100 g) **breadcrumbs**

FOR TOPPING

1 **large egg, lightly beaten**

Confectioners' sugar, for dusting

Whipped cream, if desired

Method

For the dough: On a clean work surface, combine the flour, water, oil, and a pinch of salt; knead until the dough is smooth. Form it into a ball, cover with lightly oiled plastic wrap, and let rest for at least 30 minutes.

Meanwhile, prepare the filling: Peel and slice the apples. Soak the raisins in lukewarm water for 15 minutes; drain and squeeze out excess water.

In a skillet over medium heat, melt the butter and sauté the apple slices, raisins, pine nuts, and a pinch of cinnamon. Add just enough breadcrumbs to hold the mixture together.

Heat the oven to 350°F (175°C).

On a lightly floured work surface, roll the dough into a thin rectangle, 12 by 8 inches (30 1/2 by 5 cm), then stretch it with your hands.

Spoon the filling along the long side of the pastry, leaving a 2-inch (5 cm) border. Roll the dough over the filling into a log, making sure it is well sealed by pressing down along the edges with your fingers and curling up the short ends.

Brush the strudel with the egg, place in a parchment-lined baking pan, and bake until it is golden brown (about 20 minutes), dusting with confectioners' sugar a few minutes before removing from the oven. Serve with whipped cream, if desired.

Difficulty

ANGEL WINGS

CHIACCHIERE

Preparation time: 30 minutes + 30 minutes resting time + 3 minutes cooking time

4 Servings

2 cups (250 g) **all-purpose flour**
1/3 tsp. (1 1/2 g) **baking powder**
Salt
1 **large egg**
1 1/2 tbsp. (25 g) **unsalted butter,
  melted and cooled**
2 1/2 tbsp. (20 g) **confectioners' sugar,
  plus more for dusting**
3 1/2 tbsp. (50 g) **milk**
1 tbsp. (15 ml) **grappa**
1 tsp. (5 ml) **vanilla extract**
Zest of 1/2 **lemon, grated**
**Vegetable oil, for frying and plastic
  wrap**

Method

Sift together the flour, baking powder, and a pinch of salt into a bowl.

In a large bowl, whisk the egg, butter, sugar, milk, grappa, vanilla, and lemon zest. Add the flour mixture to the egg mixture gradually, kneading until the dough is smooth. Form the dough into a ball, cover with lightly oiled plastic wrap, and let it rest for at least 30 minutes.

On a clean work surface (or using a pasta machine), roll the dough out into thin sheets, about 1/8 inch (3 mm) thick.

Cut the pastry into rectangles or diamond shapes with a pastry cutter. To obtain the characteristic wing shape, make three incisions lengthwise in each pastry rectangle or diamond. Fold the upper corner of the rectangle (or the upper corner of the diamond) and insert it into the center incision.

Heat at least 1 inch of vegetable oil in a large pot until hot and shimmering. Fry the dough for about 3 minutes and drain it on paper towels.

Dust with confectioners' sugar before serving.

Difficulty

ITALIAN CROISSANTS
CORNETTI ALL'ITALIANA

Preparation time: 1 hour + 2 1/2 hours rising time + 18 minutes cooking time

4 to 6 Servings

FOR THE DOUGH

2 cups (250 g) **all-purpose flour**
1 1/2 tsp. (10 g) **active dry yeast**
1/2 cup (100 ml) **water**
1/4 cup (45 g) **sugar**
1 **large egg**
3/4 tsp. (5 g) **honey**
Vanilla extract
Zest of 1 **lemon, grated**
3 1/2 tbsp. (50 g) **unsalted butter, room temperature**
1/2 tsp. (3 g) **salt**

FOR THE BUTTER MIXTURE

1/2 cup (125 g) **unsalted butter, room temperature**
3 tbsp. plus 1/2 tsp. (25 g) **all-purpose flour**

CHOICES FOR THE FILLING

10 tbsp. (200 g) **jam**
12 tbsp. (200 g) **chocolate cream**

FOR TOPPING

1 **large egg, lightly beaten**
Very dense sugar syrup or confectioners' sugar (optional)

Difficulty

Method

For the batter: Mix 1 cup flour with the yeast and just over 1/4 cup (60 ml) water. Let rise for 30 minutes.

Add the sugar, egg, honey, a dash of vanilla, and the lemon zest; mix well, adding just over 8 tsp. (40 ml) water. Add the butter and salt and knead the dough until it becomes smooth and elastic.

Form the dough into a ball and cover in plastic wrap. Refrigerate for 30 minutes.

For the butter mixture: Mix the butter with the flour. Refrigerate for 30 minutes to set until the dough is ready.

On a clean, lightly floured surface, roll out the dough into a 8-by-16-inch (20-by-40-cm) rectangle. Place the butter mixture on the rectangle and wrap the dough around it, then roll out the butter-enclosed dough to about 3/4 inch (2 cm) thick, then fold into thirds.

Roll it out again, this time in the opposite direction, and fold it again into thirds. Wrap in plastic and refrigerate for 30 minutes.

Repeat 2 more times, each time folding the dough into thirds.

When ready to bake the croissants, heat the oven to 425°F (220°C).

Roll out the dough to about 1/8 inch (3 mm) thick and cut into triangles. Spoon 1 1/2 tsp. (10 g) of jam or chocolate cream on the short side of each triangle and then roll up the croissants.

Arrange the croissants on parchment-lined baking sheets and let rise in a warm place for 90 minutes.

Brush the surface of the croissants with the beaten egg and bake for 17 to 18 minutes. Brush the croissants with the dense sugar syrup, or dust with confectioners' sugar.

HONEY FRITTERS
STRUFFOLI

Preparation time: 30 minutes + 5 minutes cooking time

4 Servings

FOR THE PASTRY
2 1/2 cups (300 g) **all-purpose flour,
plus more for dusting**
1/3 stick (40 g) **unsalted butter, room
temperature**
2 tbsp. (25 g) **sugar**
1 pinch **salt**
1 pinch **baking soda**
1 tbsp. (15 ml) **milk**
2 **large eggs plus** 1 **egg yolk**
1 tbsp. **anisette liqueur**

FOR THE GLAZE
2/3 cup (225 g) **honey**
1 oz. (30 g) **candied orange peel**
1/3 oz. (10 g) **colored candies
(Italian *diavolilli* or sprinkles)**

Vegetable oil, for frying

Method

For the pastry: In a very large bowl or on a clean work surface, make a well in the flour. Add all the remaining pastry ingredients to the well.

Using a fork or your hands, mix the ingredients at the center of the well. Gradually incorporate the flour, kneading until you obtain a soft, uniform dough. (If the dough is too soft, add flour. If it is too dry, add milk.)

Continue to knead for another 5 to 6 minutes, then cover the bowl with a cloth and let the dough rest for at least 15 minutes.

Divide the dough and roll it into long cylindrical strips about 1/2 inch (1 cm) in diameter. Make the *struffoli* by cutting the strips into pieces of dough approximately 1/2 inch (1 cm) long. Roll pieces into balls and place on a floured tray.

In a large, deep pot, heat the oil to 375°F (190°C). Working in batches to avoid crowding the pan, fry the balls until dark golden brown, using a slotted spoon to turn them often (they will puff up while cooking). As they finish, transfer them to a paper-towel-lined tray to drain.

For the glaze: Bring the honey to a simmer in a large saucepan over medium heat. As soon as the honey begins to boil, add the orange peel and stir to combine.

Cook for 1 to 2 minutes until the honey begins to foam. Remove the saucepan from the heat and, working in batches, add the *struffoli*. Stir gently, being careful to keep the *struffoli* from sticking. Immediately transfer them to a plate to cool.

Sprinkle the *struffoli* with the candied almonds.

Serve at room temperature.

Difficulty

BRIOCHED ROSE CAKE

TORTA DI ROSE BRIOSCIATA

Preparation time: 40 minutes + 2 hours rising time + 30 minutes cooking time

4 to 6 Servings

FOR THE ROSE CAKE

2 cups (250 g) **all-purpose flour, plus more for surface**

1 tsp. (3 g) **active dry yeast**

2/3 cup (150 ml) **water**

1/4 cup (50 g) **sugar**

3 **egg yolks**

Zest of 1 **lemon, grated**

Vanilla extract

1/4 cup plus 1 tbsp. (75 ml) **milk**

1/4 cup plus 1 3/4 tsp. (65 g) **butter, room temperature, plus more for pan**

1/2 tsp. (2.5 g) **salt**

FOR FILLING AND GLAZE

7 oz. (200 g) **pastry cream (see p. 16)**

1 large egg, lightly beaten

7 1/2 tsp. (50 g) **apricot jelly**

Method

For the dough: Mix 1 cup of flour with the yeast and water (as needed).

Add the remaining 1 cup of flour, along with the sugar, egg yolks, lemon zest, a dash of vanilla, and the milk (as needed); mix well. Lastly, add the butter and salt and knead until the dough becomes smooth and elastic.

Form the dough into a ball, place it on a floured surface, cover, and let rest until the leavening begins. When the dough begins to visibly expand (after 20 to 30 minutes), fold it over itself, and roll it out into a rectangle between 1/4 and 1/8 inch (5 mm) thick.

Spread the dough with the pastry cream, roll it up, and cut it into slices a bit taller than the cake pan you will use for baking.

Butter and flour a cake pan. Arrange the dough slices vertically in the pan and let them rise in a warm place for about 1 hour.

Heat the oven to 350°F (180°C).

Brush the surface of the dough with the beaten egg and bake for about 30 minutes, or until golden brown.

Remove the cake from the oven.

For the glaze: In a saucepan, warm the apricot jelly over medium low. Brush apricot jelly glaze on the surface of the cake.

Difficulty

FRIED TORTELLI

TORTELLI FRITTI

Preparation time: 40 minutes + 2 hours rising time + 5 minutes cooking time

4 to 6 Servings

3/4 tsp. (3 g) **active dry yeast**
1/4 cup (50 ml) **milk, room temperature**
5 oz. (125 g) **potatoes, about 1 medium**
2 cups (250 g) **all-purpose flour, plus more for dusting**
1 **large egg**
2 1/2 tsp. (10 g) **granulated sugar**
Salt
1 3/4 tbsp. (25 g) **unsalted butter, room temperature**
Vegetable oil, for frying
1/2 cup plus 2 tbsp. (200 g) **jam (preferably cherry or plum)**
Confectioners' sugar, for dusting

Method

Dissolve the yeast in 2 tbsp. of milk and set aside.

Scrub and boil the potatoes, leaving the skins on, until tender, about 15 minutes.

Run the potatoes through a potato ricer and let cool.

In a large bowl, mix together the yeast mixture, potatoes, flour, egg, granulated sugar, and a pinch of salt. Add the remaining 2 tablespoons of milk and continue kneading the dough. Lastly, add the butter and a pinch of salt, kneading until you have a smooth, elastic dough.

Cover the dough and let it rise, for at least 1 hour, at room temperature.

On a clean, lightly floured work surface, roll out the dough to between 1/4 and 1/8 inch (1/2 cm) thick. Cut dough in half.

Spacing evenly, place 1 teaspoon of jam on half of the rolled-out dough.

Cover with the other half of the dough and use a pasta cutter to cut out rectangular tortelli.

Arrange them on a baking sheet, cover with a floured cloth, and let rise in a warm place until doubled in volume (about 1 hour).

In a large, deep pot, heat the oil to 375°F (190°C). Working in batches to avoid crowding, fry the tortelli until golden.

Remove the tortelli with a slotted spoon and place on paper towels to drain, then dust with confectioners' sugar.

Difficulty

VENETIANS
VENEZIANE

Preparation time: 40 minutes + 2 hours for rising + 17 to 18 minutes cooking time

4 to 6 Servings

FOR THE VENETIANS DOUGH

2 cups (250 g) **all-purpose flour, plus more for dusting**

3/4 tsp. (3 g) **active dry yeast**

1/2 cup (100 ml) **lukewarm water**

1/4 cup (50 g) **sugar**

1 **large egg**

Zest of 1 **lemon, grated**

Vanilla extract

3 1/2 tbsp. (50 g) **unsalted butter, room temperature**

1/2 tsp. (3 g) **salt**

FOR THE GLAZE

1 **large egg, lightly beaten**

9 oz. (250 g) **pastry cream** (see p. 16)

Sanding sugar

Method

For the dough: Mix 1 cup of flour with the yeast and 1/4 cup of water in a large bowl. Let rise for 30 minutes.

Add the remaining 1 cup of flour, along with the sugar, egg, lemon zest, a dash of vanilla, and the remaining water (as needed); mix well. Lastly, add the butter and salt, and knead until the dough becomes smooth and elastic.

Form the dough into a ball, place it on a floured surface, cover, and let rest until the leavening begins.

When the dough begins to visibly expand (after 20 to 30 minutes), fold it over itself, divide it into portions of about 3 ounces (85 g) each, and roll each portion into a well-formed ball.

Arrange the balls, well-spaced, on parchment-lined baking sheets and let rise in a warm place for about 90 minutes.

Heat the oven to 425°F (220°C).

Glaze the Venetians with the beaten egg.

Use a pastry bag to pipe a spiral of pastry cream on top of each Venetian. Sprinkle with sugar.

Bake for 17 to 18 minutes.

Difficulty

RAISIN TWISTS
TRECCE ALL'UVETTA

Preparation time: 30 minutes + 30 minutes resting time + 2 1/2 hours rising time + 18 to 20 minutes cooking time

4 to 6 Servings

FOR THE VENETIANS DOUGH

2 cups (250 g) **all-purpose flour, plus more for dusting**
3/4 tsp. (3 g) **active dry yeast**
1/2 cup (100 ml) **lukewarm water**
1/4 cup (50 g) **sugar**
1 **large egg**
Zest of 1 **lemon, grated**
Vanilla extract
3 1/2 tbsp. (50 g) **unsalted butter, room temperature**
1/2 tsp. (3 g) **salt**

FOR FILLING AND TOPPINGS

7 oz. (200 g) **puff pastry dough (see p. 26)**
3 1/2 oz. (100 g) **pastry cream (see p. 16) or jam**
1 oz. (30 g) **raisins, or** about 1/4 cup

FOR GLAZE

1 **large egg, lightly beaten**
Sanding sugar

Method

For the dough: Mix 1 cup of flour with the yeast and 1/4 cup of water in a large bowl. Let rise for 30 minutes.

Add the remaining 1 cup of flour, along with the sugar, egg, lemon zest, a dash of vanilla, and the remaining water (as needed); mix well. Lastly, add the butter and salt, and knead until the dough becomes smooth and elastic.

Form the dough into a ball, place it on a floured surface, cover, and let rest until the leavening begins and the dough begins to visibly expand (20 to 30 minutes).

On a clean, lightly floured surface, roll out a rectangle of Venetians dough to between 1/8 and 1/4 inch (5 mm) thick. Place a rectangle of puff pastry dough that is the same size and about 1/8 inch (3 mm) thick on top of the Venetians dough. Fold dough combination into thirds and refrigerate for about 30 minutes.

Roll out the dough to about 1/8 inch (3 mm) thick, spread it with the pastry cream or jam, and sprinkle some raisins on top.

Fold the dough in half, cut it into strips just under 1 1/4 inches (3 cm) wide, and twist the strips together.

Arrange the raisin twists, well-spaced, on parchment-lined baking sheets and let rise in a warm place for about 30 minutes.

Heat the oven to 425°F (220°C).

Brush the twists with the beaten egg and sprinkle them with sugar.

Bake for 18 to 20 minutes, or until golden brown.

Difficulty

SAINT JOSEPH'S FRITTERS

ZEPPOLE

Preparation time: 40 minutes + 1 1/2 hours rising time + 5 minutes cooking time

4 to 6 Servings

FOR THE FRITTERS
1/4 cup (60 g) **unsalted butter**
3/4 cup plus 4 1/2 tsp. (200 ml) **water**
1/2 tsp. (4 g) **salt**
4 3/4 tsp. (20 g) **sugar**
1 1/2 cups (160 g) **all-purpose flour**
4 **large eggs**
Vegetable oil, for frying

FOR THE FILLING AND TOPPINGS
Pastry cream (see p. 16)
Sour cherries in syrup
Confectioners' sugar

Method

In a saucepan, melt the butter in the water with the salt and sugar and bring the mixture to a boil.

Add the flour all at once and mix over the heat, letting the resulting dough dry out until it pulls away from the sides of the saucepan.

Transfer the dough to a bowl and add the eggs, one at a time, mixing well.

Use a pastry bag fitted with a notched tip to shape rings of dough onto small square pieces of parchment.

In a large, deep pot, heat the oil to 375°F (190°C). Remove the parchment from the dough rings and immerse the rings in the oil. Fry the zeppole fritters until golden.

Remove the fritters with a slotted spoon, drain, and place them on paper towels. Use a pastry bag to fill the fritters with pastry cream, top with sour cherries in syrup, and dust them with confectioners' sugar.

Difficulty

Saint Joseph: from Carpenter to Fritter Seller?

Zeppole fritters, also called Saint Joseph's, apparently date to the first century A.D. In ancient Rome, there was a widespread belief that in order to support Mary and Jesus during the flight into Egypt, Saint Joseph sold fritters. Although this legend is far from verifiable, it is very appealing because it shows an especially human side of Joseph. Now the fritters are usually prepared on Father's Day.

LAVENDER CREAM IN A CRISPY ROLL
CREMOSO DI LAVANDA SU CILINDRO CROCCANTE

Preparation time: 40 minutes + 5 hours chilling time

4 Servings

FOR THE LAVENDER CREAM

2 sheets (4 g) **gelatin, or** 1/2 envelope granulated gelatin

1 cup (250 g) **sweetened light cream**

1 tbsp. (20 g) **lavender flowers**

3 **large eggs, separated**

1/2 cup (100 g) **superfine sugar**

FOR THE SUGAR ROLLS

2 cups (500 g) **freshly squeezed orange juice**

1/4 cup (50 g) **superfine sugar**

1/3 cup (50 g) **all-purpose flour**

3 tbsp. (50 g) **unsalted butter, room temperature**

FOR THE SAUCE

2 **pink grapefruits**

1/4 cup (50 g) **sugar, plus more for blanching zest**

3/4 tsp. (4 g) **cornstarch**

Lavender flowers, plus more for garnish

Lemon thyme

Difficulty

Method

For lavender cream: Soak gelatin sheets in cold water; drain and squeeze them dry.

In a saucepan over medium heat, bring 1/2 cup (125 g) of cream to a boil with the lavender flowers. Simmer for 2 minutes. Strain mixture and let cool.

Beat egg yolks and sugar in a metal bowl. Add lavender cream and return to heat. Simmer, whisking constantly until thickened, heating to 176°F (80°C) on a candy thermometer for 2 minutes.

Add gelatin; stir to combine. Let cool to room temperature. Beat egg whites to stiff peaks; fold into lavender mixture.

Whip the remaining 1/2 cup cream and fold into mixture. Spoon into a disposable pastry bag. Refrigerate for 5 hours.

For sugar rolls: Mix all ingredients together in a bowl. Cover with plastic wrap and refrigerate for 1 hour.

When ready for baking, heat oven to 350°F (180°C). Spread sugar roll mixture evenly on a parchment-lined baking sheet, making 4 strips measuring 4 by 2 1/2 inches (10 by 6 cm) each. Bake for 6 minutes. Remove from oven. Trim with a knife, roll into cylinders, and leave to cool and dry.

For sauce: Zest grapefruits, discarding white pith. In a saucepan, blanch zest in water and sugar. Strain zest and repeat blanching.

Juice the grapefruit and strain juice. Heat grapefruit juice and pulp with the sugar in a saucepan. Reduce over low heat.

Add cornstarch and adjust the density with water, whisking to thicken to a dense liquid. Add a few lavender flowers, lemon thyme, and grapefruit zest.

To serve, fill rolls using a pastry bag with lavender cream. Drizzle sauce over each roll and garnish with a lavender flower.

POTATO DOUGHNUTS
BOMBOLONI CON PATATE

Preparation time: 40 minutes + 1 hour 30 minutes rising time + 5 minutes cooking time

4 Servings

1/2 lb. (250 g) **potatoes, about 2 medium**

1 1/2 tsp. (4 g) **active dry yeast**

1/3 cup plus 1 1/2 tbsp. (100 ml) **milk**

4 cups (500 g) **all-purpose flour, plus more for dusting**

2 **large eggs**

1 1/2 tsp. (10 g) **sugar, plus more for dusting**

3 1/2 tbsp. (50 g) **unsalted butter, room temperature**

Salt

Vegetable oil, for frying

Method

Scrub and boil the potatoes, with skins on, until tender, about 15 minutes. Mash the potatoes with a potato ricer and let them cool.

Dissolve the yeast in 2 tbsp. of the milk.

Mix the flour with the mashed potatoes. Add the yeast mixture, the eggs, and the sugar. Mix in the remaining milk. Lastly, mix in the butter and a pinch of salt and knead until the dough becomes smooth and elastic. Cover the dough and let rise for about 30 minutes.

On a clean, lightly floured surface, roll out the dough to about 3/4 inch (2 cm) thick. Using a pastry ring, cut the dough into 4-inch (10 cm) rounds. Place the dough rounds onto a baking sheet. Cover with a floured towel and let rise until doubled in volume (at least 1 hour).

In a large, deep pot, heat the oil to 375°F (190°C) on a deep-fry or candy thermometer. Fry the doughnuts until golden. Remove doughnuts with a slotted spoon, drain, and place on paper towels. Dust with sugar.

Difficulty

CREAMY AND FROZEN DESSERTS

CHAPTER FIVE

SICILIAN CHEESECAKE

CASSATA

Preparation time: 1 hour + 3 hours resting time

4 Servings

FOR THE CAKE AND RICOTTA CREAM

9 oz. (250 g) **sheep's-milk ricotta**

1/2 cup (90 g) **sugar**

1 oz. (25 g) **candied orange peel, diced,
plus more for decorating**

1 oz. (25 g) **dark chocolate, chopped**

7 oz. (200 g) **sponge cake (see p. 20)**

FOR THE MARASCHINO SYRUP

4 1/2 tbsp. (65 ml) **water**

2/3 cup (125 g) **sugar**

3 tbsp. (40 ml) **maraschino cherry
liqueur**

FOR THE ICING

1 cup (100 g) **confectioners' sugar,
sifted**

1 tbsp. (15 ml) **water**

2-3 drops **lemon juice**

Green food coloring, as needed

3 1/2 oz. (100 g) **marzipan**

Difficulty

Method

For the ricotta cream: Strain the ricotta in a sieve, then transfer to a bowl and cream with the sugar. Add the candied orange peel and the chocolate and stir. Line the inside of a 9-inch cake pan or dessert mold with plastic wrap or waxed paper, leaving a 3-inch overhang. Cut the sponge cake into 2 layers and place 1 layer on the bottom of the dessert mold.

For the maraschino syrup: Bring the water and the sugar to a boil in a saucepan. Cook until the sugar has dissolved, then cool. When the syrup has cooled to lukewarm, combine with the cherry liqueur. Pour the syrup on both layers of the sponge cake to soak.

Spoon the ricotta cream over the sponge cake in the pan, spreading evenly. Place the other layer of moistened sponge cake on top and cover. Refrigerate the cake for several hours.

For the icing: Beat together the confectioners' sugar, water, and lemon juice until well combined.

Using the overhang of plastic wrap or waxed paper, remove the cake from the mold. Spread icing over top and sides.

Add a few drops of green food coloring to the marzipan, if desired. Roll out the marzipan with a rolling pin to a thickness of about 1/16 inch (1 mm).

Wrap the sides of the cassata with the marzipan and trim the edges. Decorate with candied orange peel, if desired.

PISTACHIO ICE CREAM WITH DRIED FIGS IN MARSALA

GELATO DI PISTACCHIO CON FICHI SECCHI AL MARSALA

Preparation time: 1 hour 30 minutes + 6 hours freezing time

4 Servings

FOR THE ICE CREAM

3/4 cup plus 1 1/2 tbsp. (200 ml) **milk**

1/4 **vanilla bean, halved lengthwise, seeds scraped**

1 **large egg yolk**

3 tbsp. (40 g) **granulated sugar**

0.7 oz. (20 g) **unsweetened pistachio paste** (about 1 1/2 tbsp.)

FOR THE WAFER BOWLS

3 1/2 tbsp. (50 g) **unsalted butter, room temperature**

3/8 cup (50 g) **confectioners' sugar**

3/8 cup (50 g) **all-purpose flour**

Half an egg white

1 tbsp. plus 1/2 tsp. (25 g) **honey**

FOR THE FIGS

1/4 cup (50 g) **granulated sugar**

2/3 cup (150 ml) **Marsala wine**

4 oz. (120 g) **dried figs** (about 3/4 cup)

FOR THE GARNISH

White chocolate shavings

4 **fresh mint leaves**

Difficulty

Method

For the ice cream: Combine the milk with the vanilla bean in a bowl.

With an electric mixer, beat the egg yolk and sugar together, then mix in the pistachio paste.

Gradually add the vanilla milk to the egg-sugar mixture, stirring vigorously, and heat the mixture over low heat or in a double boiler until it reaches 185°F (85°C) on an instant-read thermometer.

Cool rapidly to 40°F (4°C) by putting the mixture in a container and immersing it in a bowl of ice water. Refrigerate the ice cream base for 6 hours, then process in an ice cream maker according to manufacturer's instructions. Transfer the ice cream to an airtight container and place in freezer until firm.

For the wafer bowls: Cream the butter and sugar until the mixture is light and fluffy. Mix in the remaining ingredients, a little at a time, until a soft dough forms.

Heat the oven to 350°F (175°C). Place 4 portions of about 1 1/2 ounces (40 g) each on a parchment-lined baking sheet and, using your fingers or the back of a spoon, spread them into large rounds. Bake them for about 15 minutes, or until they start to turn light brown.

Remove them from the oven and let them cool for a few seconds. With a spatula, place each wafer over an upside-down ramekin so it takes on a bowl shape.

For the figs in syrup: Warm the sugar and Marsala together in a saucepan until the sugar dissolves. Dice the figs and add them to the syrup, then let the mixture cool.

Serve the ice cream in the wafer bowls, topped with the fig syrup. Garnish with white chocolate shavings and fresh mint leaves.

WHITE CHOCOLATE MOUSSE WITH PEACH JELLY
MOUSSE AL CIOCCOLATO BIANCO CON GELATINA DI PESCHE

Preparation time: 1 hour 30 minutes + 2 hours chilling time

4 Servings

FOR THE PEACH JELLY
3 (8 g) **gelatin sheets or** 3/4 envelope **granulated gelatin**
9 oz. (250 g) **yellow peaches, peeled, pitted, and cut into small pieces**
1/3 cup (75 g) **sugar**

FOR THE MOUSSE
9 oz. (250 g) **white chocolate, chopped, plus shavings for garnish (optional)**
1/2 cup (125 ml) **heavy cream**
11 1/2 oz. (325 g) **semi-whipped cream**

Method

For the peach jelly: Soften the gelatin sheets in cold water, then squeeze out excess liquid. (If you are using granulated gelatin, dissolve it directly in the hot peach purée.)

Purée the peaches in a blender. In a saucepan, bring the sugar and one-third of the peach purée to a boil. Dissolve the gelatin in the peach mixture. Add the remaining peach purée and stir to combine. Pour the jelly into individual serving cups or bowls and let cool.

For the mousse: Put the chocolate in a bowl. Boil the heavy cream in a saucepan and pour over the chocolate, stirring until it is smooth and creamy. Cool to 85°F (30°C) on an instant-read thermometer.

Meanwhile, to prepare the semi-whipped cream, whip the cream until soft peaks form.

Gently fold the semi-whipped cream into the cream and chocolate mixture.

Top the servings of peach jelly with the mousse. Refrigerate for at least 2 hours. Garnish with shavings of white chocolate, if desired.

Difficulty

CHESTNUT AND CHOCOLATE PUDDING

CASTAGNE AL CUCCHIAIO

Preparation time: 25 minutes + 4 hours cooling time

4 Servings

1 tbsp. (20 g) **salt**
1 1/3 lb. (600 g) **fresh or dried chestnuts**
5 oz. (150 g) **dark chocolate, chopped**
1 stick plus 1/2 tbsp. (120 g) **unsalted butter, room temperature, plus more for parchment**
1/2 cup plus 1 1/2 tbsp. (120 g) **sugar**
Heavy cream, for serving

Method

Bring a pot of salted water to a boil. If using dried chestnuts, soak in the boiling-hot salted water for 1 hour; drain. If using fresh chestnuts, simmer the nuts in the hot water for 15 to 20 minutes, cool slightly, and peel. Run the cooked chestnuts through a sieve.

Melt the chocolate in a heatproof bowl set over (not in) a pan of simmering water (or in a double boiler). Add the chocolate to the warm chestnuts together with the butter and sugar. Stir the mixture until well combined.

Line a rectangular mold with parchment and butter the parchment. Spread the chestnut mixture in the mold, level it, and cover with more parchment.

Refrigerate for at least 4 hours. When the pudding has hardened, cut into the shapes of your choice (squares, hearts, flowers, etc.). Serve with a drizzle of cream.

Difficulty

LEMON GRANITA
GRANITA AL LIMONE

Preparation time: 15 minutes + 2 to 4 hours freezing time

4 Servings

1/4 cup plus 2 tbsp. (75 g) **sugar**
1 cup (250 ml) **water**
1/2 cup (100 ml) **fresh lemon juice, strained**

Method

Prepare a syrup by bringing the sugar and water to a boil; let boil for 1 minute.

Let cool and add the lemon juice.

Freeze the liquid for about 1 hour, until ice crystals begin to form. Whisk it well and return it to the freezer. Repeat this process at least 4 or 5 times. The granita is ready when the ice reaches a uniform consistency and granularity.

Remove from the freezer and serve in 4 individual dishes.

Granitas, from the "Nivieri" to the "Pozzetto"

The granita is a cold dessert that is typical of Sicilian sweets. It is traditionally a semi-liquid concoction of water, sugar, and fresh lemon juice. The origins of the granita date to the Arabian domination of the island. The Arabs introduced an iced drink flavored with fruit juice or rosewater, often prepared with the snow collected in the winter on Mount Etna and kept in "nivieri," or freezers built of stone in natural recesses. It was not until the sixteenth century that snow began to be used as a cooling ingredient, and was used together with sea salt to keep the iced drink cool in a "pozzetto," a wooden tub with a metal bucket inside, the precursor to the modern refrigerator. The typical Sicilian granita comes in many flavors other than lemon: coffee, almond, pistachio, jasmine, cinnamon, black mulberry, and chocolate among them.

Difficulty

CHOCOLATE GRANITA

GRANITA AL CIOCCOLATO

Preparation time: 1 hour + 4 hours chilling time

4 Servings

1 1/2 cups (400 ml) **water**
1/4 cup (25 g) **cocoa powder**
3/8 cup (80 g) **sugar**

Method

Bring the water to a boil in a saucepan.

Mix the cocoa and sugar together, then whisk the mixture into the boiling water.

Let the mixture cool.

Freeze the liquid for about 1 hour, until ice crystals begin to form. Whisk it well and return it to the freezer. Repeat this process at least 4 or 5 times. The granita is ready when the ice reaches a uniform consistency and granularity.

Remove from the freezer and serve in 4 individual dishes.

Difficulty

CHOCOLATE AND MINT PARFAITS

BICCHIERINI CIOCCOLATO E MENTA

Preparation time: 30 minutes + 2 hours cooling time

4 Servings

3 sheets (7 g) **gelatin, or** 3/4 envelope
  granulated gelatin
1 cup (250 ml) **milk**
1 cup (250 ml) **heavy cream**
3/4 cup (150 g) **sugar**
1 tsp. (5 ml) **peppermint essence**
Green food coloring
1 oz. (25 g) **dark chocolate, chopped**

Method

Soak the gelatin sheets in water, then squeeze out any excess moisture.

In a medium pan, bring the milk and cream to a boil with the sugar.

Reduce the heat to low; add the gelatin sheets (or granulated gelatin) and let dissolve.

Divide this panna cotta mixture into 3 parts. Leave the first neutral. Flavor the second with the peppermint essence and color it with a few drops of green food coloring. To the final third, add the chocolate.

Strain a layer of the neutral cream into 4 dessert glasses and refrigerate to let thicken.

Pour in a layer of the mint cream and refrigerate to let it thicken (if it is too thick to pour, heat it gently to liquefy it).

Finally add the chocolate panna cotta.

Refrigerate the parfaits until ready to serve.

Difficulty

BONET (PIEDMONTESE PUDDING)

BONET

Preparation time: 20 minutes + 45 minutes cooking time + 2 hours cooling time

4 to 6 Servings

FOR THE CARAMEL
1/2 cup (100 g) **sugar**
2 tbsp. (25 ml) **water**

FOR THE PUDDING
1 1/2 cups (375 ml) **milk**
3 oz. (75 g) **amaretti cookies (about
10 cookies)**
3 **large eggs**
1/2 cup (115 g) **sugar**
1/4 cup (25 g) **unsweetened cocoa
powder**
1 tsp. (5 ml) **rum**

Method

Heat the oven to 325°F (160°C).

For the caramel: In a pan over medium heat, gently cook the sugar with the water until it turns a deep blonde color, then pour it into a dessert mold or individual molds and let cool.

For the pudding: In another saucepan, boil the milk.

Meanwhile, place the amaretti cookies between 2 sheets of waxed paper and crush into crumbs with a rolling pin.

Whisk together the eggs and sugar in a bowl, then add the amaretti crumbs, cocoa, and rum. Add the boiling milk, stir, and pour into the caramelized molds.

Prepare a hot water bath (bain-marie): Place molds in a deep baking pan and add enough hot water to the pan to reach halfway up molds. Bake in the oven for about 45 minutes.

Let the puddings cool in the refrigerator for least 2 hours before you unmold them.

TIP: *Let the puddings cool well before turning them out of the molds. They taste better when eaten the day after they're made.*

Difficulty

MILK CHOCOLATE MOUSSE
MOUSSE AL CIOCCOLATO AL LATTE

Preparation time: 1 hour 20 minutes + 3 hours cooling time

6 Servings

FOR THE CHOCOLATE CRUST

2/3 cup (80 g) **all-purpose flour**

2 1/2 tbsp. (20 g) **cornstarch**

3 tbsp. (15 g) **unsweetened cocoa powder**

3 **large eggs, separated, plus 1 large egg yolk**

1/2 cup (100 g) **sugar**

FOR THE MOUSSE

9 oz. (250 g) **milk chocolate, chopped, plus shavings for garnish**

4 (10 g) **gelatin sheets, or** 1 envelope **granulated gelatin (1/4 oz.)**

2 **large egg yolks**

1 cup (250 ml) **milk**

7 oz. (200 g) **heavy cream**

FOR THE SYRUP

2 tbsp. (30 ml) **water**

3/8 cup (80 g) **sugar**

2 1/2 tbsp. (35 ml) **rum (or other liqueur of your choice)**

Difficulty

Method

Heat the oven to 450°F (230°C).

For the chocolate crust: Sift together the flour, cornstarch, and cocoa.

With an electric mixer, beat the egg whites with the sugar in a clean bowl until soft peaks form. In a separate bowl, whisk the egg yolks until pale and fluffy. Fold the whites into the yolks, followed by the flour mixture.

Spread a layer of dough about 3/8 inch (1 cm) thick on a 12-inch baking sheet lined with parchment. Bake for 5 to 7 minutes.

For the mousse: Put the chocolate in a bowl.

If you are using gelatin sheets, soak them in cold water until softened, then squeeze out excess liquid.

In a saucepan over low heat, combine the egg yolks and milk and heat to 185°F (85°C) on a candy thermometer, stirring constantly.

Remove from the heat and add the gelatin, stirring to dissolve. Immediately pour this mixture into the chocolate and stir until smooth. Let cool to 85°F (30°C).

For the syrup: Boil the water and sugar in a pan. Let it cool, then stir in the rum.

Whip the cream until soft peaks form, then gently fold into the chocolate-mousse mixture.

Line the bottom and sides of a cake ring with the baked crust, trim the excess, and pour enough syrup on crust to soak it. Fill the crust with mousse. Smooth the surface with a spatula and refrigerate for at least 3 hours.

Remove from the pan and garnish with shaved chocolate, if desired.

LEMON MOUSSE WITH EXTRA-VIRGIN OLIVE OIL

MOUSSE DI LIMONI CON OLIO EXTRAVERGINE DI OLIVA

Preparation time: 30 minutes + 2 hours to set

4 Servings

FOR THE MERINGUE
1 tbsp. plus 1 tsp. (20 ml) **water**
1/4 cup plus 2 1/2 tbsp. (80 g) **sugar**
2 tbsp. plus 2 tsp. (40 g) **egg whites**

FOR THE MOUSSE
2 sheets **gelatin**
2/3 cup plus 1 tbsp. (170 ml) **heavy cream**
1/4 cup plus 2 tsp. (70 ml) **lemon juice**
1 tbsp. plus 1 tsp. (20 ml) **extra-virgin olive oil**

Method

For the meringue: Heat the water and 1/3 cup of sugar in a small pan.

With an electric mixer, beat the egg whites with the remaining sugar in a clean bowl until stiff, glossy peaks form.

When the simple sugar syrup reaches 250°F (121°C) on a candy thermometer, slowly add it to the egg whites, continuing to beat until the mixture cools.

For the mousse: Soak the gelatin sheets in cold water for 5 minutes, squeeze out excess moisture, then slowly dissolve them in a pan over low heat or in the microwave.

Whip the heavy cream and fold it into the meringue, along with the gelatin and lemon juice.

Pour the mixture into individual dessert molds and freeze for 2 hours, or until it sets.

To serve, transfer the mousse from the molds to serving plates and drizzle with the olive oil.

Difficulty

RICOTTA MOUSSE WITH ALMOND MILK

SPUMA DI RICOTTA AL LATTE DI MANDORLA

Preparation time: 1 hour + 8 hours chilling time + 3 hours freezing time

4 Servings

3 1/2 oz. (100 g) **unsalted almonds,
  or** about 1 cup, **finely ground**
1 1/4 cups (300 ml) **water**
2 **large egg yolks**
1/4 cup plus 2 tbsp. (75 g) **sugar**
2 **gelatin sheets** (5 g), **or** 1/2 envelope
  granulated gelatin (1/8 oz.)
9 oz. (250 g) **ricotta**
2/3 cup (160 ml) **heavy cream**

Method

Mix the ground almonds with the water. Refrigerate the mixture for about 8 hours to make almond milk. Strain the almond milk through cheesecloth.

Beat the yolks with the sugar and stir in 1/2 cup (125 ml) of almond milk. Transfer to a pan over medium heat and let the mixture thicken, stirring occasionally.

If you are using gelatin sheets, soak them in water until softened; squeeze out excess water. Dissolve the gelatin in the hot almond-milk mixture.

Let the mixture cool and stir in the ricotta. In a bowl, whip the cream and fold it into the ricotta mixture.

Pour into individual dessert molds and freeze for about 3 hours. Unmold and serve chilled.

Difficulty

ORANGE CREAM
CREMA DI ARANCE

Preparation time: 10 minutes + 15 minutes cooking time

4 Servings

4 large egg yolks
1/2 cup (100 g) **sugar**
5 tbsp. (40 g) **cornstarch**
2 cups (5 dl) **milk**
Juice and grated zest of 4 **oranges**

FOR TOPPING
3 1/2 tbsp. (50 ml) **cream**
Candied orange peels (optional)
Cinnamon (optional)

Method

In a medium bowl, whisk together the yolks, sugar, and cornstarch.

In a saucepan over medium heat, bring the milk to a boil. Slowly add the boiling milk to the egg mixture. Transfer the mixture back to the pan and bring to a boil, whisking constantly.

When the mixture thickens, remove from the heat and add the orange juice and zest.

Cool the mixture rapidly by immersing the pan in a bowl of ice water. Place in a bowl and refrigerate until thoroughly chilled.

Serve cold, in dessert bowls. Whip the cream and top the desserts with a dollop and a slice of candied orange peel, dusted with cinnamon, if desired.

Difficulty

FROZEN ZABAGLIONE WITH MOSCATO D'ASTI PASSITO AND MELON PURÉE

ZABAIONE GELATO AL MOSCATO D'ASTI PASSITO SU FRULLATO DI MELONE

Preparation time: 15 minutes + 10 minutes cooking time + 2 hours freezing time

4 Servings

FOR THE ZABAGLIONE

6 **large egg yolks**
1 cup (200 g) **sugar**
3/4 cup (200 ml) **Moscato d'Asti
   or other Muscat wine**
8 1/3 cups (500 g) **whipped cream**

FOR THE MELON PURÉE

1 **melon (such as cantaloupe), peeled,
   seeded, and cut into chunks**
1/4 cup (50g) **sugar**

Method

For the zabaglione: Whisk together the egg yolks and the sugar in a copper pan or a heatproof bowl until frothy.

Transfer the egg mixture to a copper pot or place the heatproof bowl over (not in) a pan of simmering water over medium-low heat. Slowly add the Moscato to the egg mixture, whisking constantly.

Bring the zabaglione to 175°F (80°C) on a candy or instant-read thermometer. When it begins to thicken, remove from the heat and let cool.

Gently fold in the whipped cream. Pour the mixture into a terrine and chill for 2 hours.

For the melon purée: Use a blender or food processor to purée the melon with the sugar.

To serve, remove the zabaglione from the terrine. Spoon a ladle of the purée into each dessert dish and arrange thin slices of the zabaglione on top.

Difficulty

SEMIFREDDO

SEMIFREDDO ALL'ITALIANA

Preparation time: 1 1/2 hours + 6 to 7 minutes cooking time + 2 hours freezing time

6 to 8 Servings

FOR THE ITALIAN MERINGUE
3 tbsp. (45 ml) **water**
3/4 cup plus 2 1/2 tbsp. (180 g) **sugar**
3 **egg whites**

FOR THE HAZELNUT MIXTURE
6 oz. (180 g) **pastry cream (see p. 16)**
1 1/2 oz. (40 g) **pure hazelnut paste**
3 oz. (80 g) **Italian meringue**
2 cups (250 g) **whipped cream**

FOR THE COFFEE MIXTURE
2 tbsp. plus 2 tsp. (8 g) **instant coffee**
1 cup **boiling water**
10 oz. (280 g) **pastry cream (see p. 16)**
4 1/2 oz. (125 g) **Italian meringue**
3 cups (375 g) **whipped cream**

7 oz. (200 g) **roll dough, divided
  into 2 disks**

FOR THE ROLL DOUGH
3 **large eggs, separated**
1/3 cup + 2 tsp. (75 g) **sugar**
just over 7 1/2 tsp. (20 g) **all-purpose flour**
just over 2 1/2 tsp. (7 g) **cornstarch**
1/2 **vanilla pod**
Zest of 1/4 **lemon**

FOR THE SYRUP
1/3 cup plus 1 tbsp. (80 g)
  sugar
2 tbsp. plus 2 tsp. (40 ml)
  rum or amaretto liqueur
2 tbsp. (30 ml) **water**

Difficulty

Method

For the Italian meringue: Heat the water and 3/4 cup plus 2 teaspoons (160 g) of the sugar in a pan (preferably copper).

Beat the egg whites with the remaining sugar until stiff peaks form.

When the simple sugar reaches 250°F (121°C) on a candy thermometer, combine it with the egg whites and continue beating until the mixture is lukewarm. Set aside.

For the hazelnut mixture: Stir together the pastry cream and the hazelnut paste, then gently add the Italian meringue. Finally, fold in the whipped cream.

For the coffee mixture: Dissolve the instant coffee in the boiling water. Add to the pastry cream and gently mix in the Italian meringue. Finally, fold in the whipped cream.

For classic roll dough: Heat the oven to 450°F (240°C). Beat the egg whites with 2 tablespoons (25 g) sugar until stiff peaks form. In a separate bowl, beat the egg yolks with the remaining 1/3 cup sugar.

Sift together the flour and the cornstarch, then add the vanilla pod (split lengthwise and seeds scraped) and the zest.

Add the egg yolk mixture to the whites and gently fold in the flour mixture.

Spread the mixture on a 12-by-15-inch (30-by-40-cm) baking sheet lined with parchment and bake for 5 to 7 minutes.

For the syrup: Combine all the ingredients in a bowl; stir to combine. Line the bottom and halfway up the sides of an 8-inch (20 cm) stainless-steel dessert mold with the roll dough. Soak dough with the syrup and fill halfway with the coffee mixture. Add the second disk of roll dough, soak it with syrup, and top with the hazelnut mixture. Smooth the surface of the dessert with a spatula and place in the freezer for 2 hours.

Remove from the mold and decorate as desired.

FRUIT SORBET

SORBETTI ALLA FRUTTA

Preparation time: 30 minutes + 6 hours chilling time

Makes about 1 quart (1 liter) of sorbet

LEMON SORBET

2 cups (440 ml) **water**
1 cup **sugar**
3/4 cup (190 ml) **lemon juice**
1 tbsp. (5 g) **lemon zest**

ORANGE SORBET

3/4 cup plus 1 tbsp. (195 ml) **water**
1 cup plus 2 tbsp. (225 g) **sugar**
1 1/2 cups (375 ml) **mandarin orange juice**
1 tbsp. (15 ml) **lemon juice**

STRAWBERRY SORBET

1 1/4 cups (300 ml) **water**
2 cups (300 g) **strawberries**
1 cup (200 g) **sugar**
Juice of 1/4 **lemon**

Method

For lemon and mandarin orange sorbets: Bring the water to a boil in a pan. Pour the sugar in a steady stream into the boiling water, whisking well until the mixture reaches 150°F (65°C) on a candy thermometer. Remove from the heat and let cool.

When the simple syrup is cool, add the lemon juice and zest for lemon sorbet or mandarin and lemon juices for orange sorbet; stir to combine. Cool rapidly to 40°F (4°C) by putting the mixture in a container and immersing it in a bowl of ice water.

Refrigerate for 6 hours, then process in an ice cream maker until thick, according to manufacturer's instructions. Transfer to an airtight container and freeze until ready to serve.

For strawberry sorbet: Bring the water to a boil in a pan. Add the strawberries to boiling water, then add the sugar in a slow stream, whisking well until the mixture reaches 150°F (65°C) on a candy thermometer. Remove from the heat and let cool.

When the simple syrup is cool, add the lemon juice. Follow the remainder of the directions for lemon and orange sorbets, above.

The Grandfather of Gelato

Sorbet, a cold dessert eaten with a spoon, is an ancestor of gelato. Made with water, fruit, sugar, and sometimes liqueur, it is not to be confused with granita. Ancient Romans enjoyed sorbets as a pleasing way to beat the summer heat. Apparently, the emperor Nero had ice brought in from the Apennines so that he could enjoy delicious, refreshing fruit sorbets.

Difficulty

TIRAMISÙ

TIRAMISÙ

Preparation time: 30 minutes + 2 hours resting time

4 Servings

4 **large egg yolks plus** 2 **large egg whites**

1/2 cup plus 2 tbsp. (125 g) **sugar**

1 cup (250 g) **mascarpone**

8 **ladyfingers** (*savoiardi*; see p. 102)

1 cup (200 ml) **sweetened coffee**

1 tbsp. plus 2 tsp. (25 ml) **brandy (optional)**

Unsweetened cocoa powder, as needed

Method

Beat the egg yolks with three-quarters of the sugar in a heatproof bowl until thick and pale, then set over (not in) a pan of simmering water until warmed through. Remove from the heat.

In another bowl, beat the egg whites with the remaining sugar until stiff peaks form.

Stir the mascarpone into the egg yolk mixture, then gently fold in the egg white mixture, letting it remain light and frothy.

Dip the ladyfingers in the sweetened coffee; add brandy, if desired. Transfer 4 ladyfingers to an 8-inch glass baking dish or 4 small dessert bowls (2 ladyfingers per bowl).

Pour in a layer of the cream mixture, alternating with another layer of ladyfingers and ending with cream.

Refrigerate the tiramisù, covered, for about 2 hours.

Top with a generous dusting of cocoa.

Delicate Mascarpone Cheese

Mascarpone is one of the fundamental ingredients in this famous creamy dessert. Tiramisù was invented in the late 1960s by the pastry chef Roberto Linguanotto at the Alle Becchiere restaurant in Treviso. This fresh cheese is made from the acid-thermal coagulation of cream through the addition of acetic or citric acid and high-temperature processing (as much as 194° to 203°F or 90° to 95°C) lasting between 5 and 10 minutes. It is typical of Lombardy, where the dialect term for cream is mascherpa. It is a soft but dense cream, ranges from white to pale yellow, and is especially mild in flavor, all characteristics that make it a perfect ingredient in many pastry creams.

Difficulty

ITALIAN GELATO CAKE

TORTA GELATO ITALIA

Preparation time: 1 hour + 18 minutes cooking time + 3 hours freezing time

4 to 6 Servings

11 oz. (300 g) **strawberry sorbet
(see p. 190)**

11 oz. (300 g) **plain gelato (see below)**

11 oz. (300 g) **pistachio gelato
(see p. 164)**

FOR PLAIN GELATO (ABOUT 2 POUNDS)
2 cups (500 ml) **milk**

1/2 cup plus 1 1/2 tbsp. (120 g) **sugar**

2 tbsp. plus 2 tsp. (20 g) **powdered
skim milk**

1/2 cup (100 ml) **heavy cream**

FOR ALMOND PISTACHIO COOKIE "CRUST"
2 **large egg whites**

4 3/4 tsp. (20 g) **superfine sugar**

1/3 cup plus 4 tsp. (50 g) **confectioners'
sugar**

2/3 cup (50 g) **raw almonds, unpeeled**

2 tbsp. (15 g) **whole almonds and
pistachios, chopped**

Difficulty

Method

For plain gelato: In a saucepan, heat milk to 115°F (45°C) on an instant-read thermometer. In a bowl, whisk together sugar and powdered milk. Whisk mixture into milk.

Heat mixture to 150°F (65°C), add cream; cook to 185°F (85°C).

Cool to 40°F (4°C) by putting mixture in a container and immersing it in ice water. Refrigerate for 6 hours. Process in an ice cream maker until thick, and dry in appearance (not shiny). Transfer to a container; freeze until firm.

For almond–pistachio cookie crust: Heat oven to 350°F (180°C).

Beat whites with superfine sugar and set aside. In a food processor, pulse confectioners' sugar and raw almonds until finely ground. Fold confectioners' sugar mixture into egg whites.

With a pastry bag, pipe cookie crust onto a parchment-lined baking sheet. Sprinkle crust with chopped almonds and pistachios. Bake for 18 minutes, or until golden brown.

Freeze three concentric half-sphere molds, the largest 7 inches (18 cm) in diameter.

Completely fill smallest mold with strawberry sorbet; smooth surface. Freeze for 1 hour. Then, run mold under cold water to loosen sorbet. Remove sorbet; return to freezer.

Line medium mold with plain gelato; fill with sorbet "dome." Smooth surface; freeze for 1 hour; remove from mold; return sorbet-gelato to freezer.

Line largest mold with pistachio gelato. Fill with sorbet-plain gelato "domes."

Cover with crust; freeze dessert for 1 hour.

Unmold and serve.

ENGLISH TRIFLE
ZUPPA INGLESE

Preparation time: 30 minutes + 1 hour resting time

4 to 6 Servings

FOR THE SYRUP

2 tbsp. (30 ml) **water**
1/3 cup plus 1 tbsp. (80 g) **sugar**
8 tsp. (40 ml) **alkermes (Tuscan spiced liqueur) or Marsala wine**

FOR THE CAKE

1 **rectangular sponge cake, weighing about** 12 oz. (350 g) **(see p. 20)**
7 oz. (200 g) **pastry cream (see p. 16)**
7 oz. (200 g) **chocolate pastry cream (see p. 16)**

FOR THE ITALIAN MERINGUE

2 tbsp. (30 ml) **water**
1/2 cup plus 2 tbsp. (125 g) **sugar**
2 **large egg whites**

Method

For the syrup: Bring the water and sugar to a boil in a saucepan.

Let cool, then add the liqueur.

For the cake: Divide the sponge cake into three layers. Soak the first layer with the syrup. Use a pastry bag to spread the plain pastry cream over the surface. Place the second layer on top, soak it with syrup, and spread it with the chocolate pastry cream. Cover with the last layer of sponge cake and soak with liqueur (if you like, you can also substitute one or more layers of plain sponge cake with chocolate sponge cake). Refrigerate for at least 1 hour.

For the Italian meringue: Heat the water and 1/2 cup plus 2 tsp. (110 g) of the sugar in a saucepan (preferably copper). Meanwhile, with an electric mixer on medium-high speed, beat the egg whites with the remaining 3 1/2 teaspoons (15 g) of sugar until stiff peaks form. When the sugar mixture reaches 250°F (121°C) on a candy thermometer, pour it in a thin stream into the egg whites and beat until cool.

Use a pastry bag fitted with a plain tip to pipe the meringue on top of the zuppa inglese. Brown the meringue using a kitchen torch.

An Emilian Delight

Zuppa inglese, a delicious traditional Italian dessert, was present in the sixteenth century among the pastries served to the dukes of Este, lords of the Ferrara, in Emilia Romagna. As its name suggests, it might derive from the English trifle, which is made of sponge cake and pastry cream and generously soaked in sherry. As in the past, zuppa inglese continues to come in infinite variations. Its base can consist of sponge cake or ladyfingers, the liqueur used can vary from a rosolio cordial to Marsala wine, and the pastry cream can be replaced by apricot jam or a fruit compote.

Difficulty

CRÈME BRÛLÉE

CRÈME BRÛLÉE

Preparation time: 15 minutes + 60 to 75 minutes cooking time + 2 hours chilling time

4 Servings

1 **vanilla bean**
2 cups (500 ml) **heavy cream**
5 **large egg yolks**
1/2 cup plus 2 tbsp. (125 g) **sugar**
3 1/2 tbsp. (40 g) **light brown sugar**

Method

Heat the oven to 200°F (100°C).

Slice the vanilla bean open lengthwise, using the tip of a sharp knife, and scrape the seeds into the cream in a medium saucepan. Bring to a boil over low heat.

In a separate bowl, beat the egg yolks with the sugar in a bowl until foamy and pale yellow.

Slowly stream the boiling cream into the egg yolk mixture, stirring well but trying to avoid forming froth.

Pour the cream into small dessert molds or ramekins. Prepare a hot water bath (bain-marie): Place the ramekins in a deep baking pan. Fill the pan with enough hot water to reach halfway up the sides of the ramekins. Bake in the oven until the cream has set, 20 to 25 minutes.

Transfer the ramekins to a wire cooling rack, cool completely, then refrigerate for at least 2 hours.

Sprinkle brown sugar on top of each crème and caramelize with a kitchen torch, or place 4 inches under a hot oven broiler until they are light brown.

Difficulty

CRÈME CARAMEL

CRÈME CARAMEL

Preparation time: 15 minutes + 35 to 40 minutes cooking time + 2 hours chilling time

4 Servings

FOR THE CARAMEL
1/4 cup (50 g) **sugar**

FOR THE CUSTARD
1 1/3 cups (330 ml) **milk**
3/8 cup (85 g) **sugar**
Zest of 1/2 **lemon**
2 **large eggs, beaten**

Method

Heat the oven to 300°F (150°C).

For the caramel: In a saucepan over medium-high heat, combine the sugar and a tablespoon of water and bring to a boil.

Reduce the heat to medium and cook until the mixture is light brown and caramelized. Divide the caramel evenly between 4 ramekins or small dessert molds, swirling to coat the ramekins. Let cool.

For the custard: In a saucepan, combine the milk, sugar, and lemon zest and bring to a boil. Remove and discard the zest.

In a bowl, add a quarter of the milk mixture to the eggs and stir well. Then add the remaining milk mixture. (This will help you avoid cooking the eggs.)

Pour the mixture into the ramekins or molds. Prepare a hot water bath (bain-marie): Place the ramekins in a deep baking pan. Fill the pan with enough hot water to reach halfway up the sides of the ramekins. Bake for 35 to 40 minutes.

Transfer the ramekins to a wire cooling rack, cool completely, then refrigerate for at least 2 hours.

Before serving, invert each mold onto a dessert plate and serve the crème with caramel on top.

Difficulty

VANILLA AND CHOCOLATE ICE CREAM
GELATO CIOCCOLATO E CREMA

Preparation time: 20 minutes + 6 hours freezing time

Makes 2 pints (900 ml) of ice cream

FOR THE CHOCOLATE
2 cups (500 ml) **milk**
3/4 cup (130 g) **sugar**
1/2 cup plus 2 tbsp. (50 g)
  unsweetened cocoa powder
3 **large egg yolks**
1/3 oz. (10 g) **dark chocolate, chopped**

FOR THE VANILLA
1/2 **vanilla bean, split lengthwise,
  seeds scraped**
2 cups (500 ml) **milk**
3/4 cup (150 g) **sugar**
2 tbsp. (15 g) **powdered skim milk**
5 **large egg yolks** (90 g)
3 1/2 tbsp. (50 ml) **heavy cream**

Method

For the chocolate: In a saucepan, heat the milk to 115°F (45°C), using an instant-read thermometer.

In a bowl, whisk together the sugar and cocoa, then pour the dry mixture into the milk; whisk again to combine.

Heat the mixture to 150°F (65°C), whisk in the egg yolks and cook, stirring, for 10 seconds. Add the dark chocolate, stirring until melted.

Cool rapidly to 40°F (4°C) by putting the mixture in a container and immersing it in a bowl of ice water.

Refrigerate the ice cream base for 6 hours, then process in an ice cream maker according to the manufacturer's instructions.

Transfer the ice cream to an airtight container and place in freezer until firm.

For the vanilla: In a saucepan, combine the vanilla bean with the milk and heat to 115°F (45°C), using an instant-read thermometer. In a bowl, whisk together the sugar and powdered milk, then gradually sprinkle the mixture into the vanilla milk, whisking to combine. Heat the mixture to 150°F (65°C).

Whisk together the egg yolks and cream, then whisk into the milk and cook, stirring, for 10 seconds.

Cool rapidly to 40°F (4°C) by putting the mixture in a container and immersing it in a bowl of ice water.

Refrigerate for 6 hours, remove the vanilla bean, then process in an ice cream maker, according to manufacturer's instructions, until thick. Transfer to an airtight container and place in the freezer until firm.

Difficulty

ITALIAN TRIFLE

ZUPPA INGLESE

Preparation time: 1 hour 30 minutes

4 Servings

FOR THE LADYFINGERS (SEE P. 102)
8 (150 g) large eggs, separated
2 tbsp. (30 g) sugar
1 1/4 cups (180 g) flour, sifted, plus more
  for baking sheet
Unsalted butter, for pans

FOR THE OLD-FASHIONED PASTRY CREAM (SEE P. 16)
1 cup (250 ml) milk
1/2 vanilla bean, halved lengthwise,
  seeds scraped
Zest of 1/2 lemon
10 (250 g) large egg yolks
3/4 cup (150 g) sugar
3 tbsp. (40 g) flour, sifted

FOR CHOCOLATE CUSTARD
2 cups (500 ml) milk
1/2 cup (100 g) egg yolks
3/4 cup (150 g) sugar
2/3 cup (100 g) unsweetened cocoa powder
3 oz. (100 g) dark chocolate, chopped

FOR THE SYRUP
1/2 cup (100 ml) water
1/2 cup (100 g) sugar
1 2/3 cup (400 ml) alkermes (Tuscan
  spiced liqueur) or Marsala wine
1 vanilla bean

FOR THE GARNISH
Liqueur-soaked cherries
Fresh fruit
Whipped cream
Chocolate, broken into
  pieces

Difficulty

Method

For ladyfingers: Heat oven to 350°F (180°C).

In a bowl, beat yolks with half the sugar. In separate bowl, beat whites with the remaining sugar. Fold in yolk mixture and flour.

Spread a 1/8-inch (0.5-cm) layer of batter on a buttered, floured baking sheet. Bake for 10 minutes.

Cut into 3/4- by 2 3/4-inch (2- by-7-cm) rectangles.

For pastry cream: In a saucepan over medium heat, bring milk to a boil with vanilla bean and lemon zest.

Beat yolks with sugar in a bowl. Add flour; mix well.

Whisk in one-quarter of hot milk. Whisk in remainder of milk.

Return mixture to pan; bring to a boil, whisking constantly, for 2 minutes, or until mixture thickens. Pour custard into a heat-proof bowl; let cool.

For chocolate custard: Bring milk to a boil in a saucepan.

Beat yolks with sugar in a bowl. Whisk a quarter of milk into eggs; stir. Whisk in remaining milk.

Return mixture to pan; bring to a boil, whisking constantly.

Add cocoa and chocolate; stir until melted and mixture thickens. Pour custard into a bowl; let cool.

For syrup: Bring the water, vanilla bean, and sugar to a boil, stirring until sugar dissolves. Remove from heat, let cool; stir in liqueur.

Assemble and serve: Soak ladyfingers in syrup. Layer as follows: Ladyfingers/pastry cream/ladyfingers/chocolate custard/ladyfingers. Cut into squares. Garnish as desired. Serve cold.

CHOCOLATE FONDUE
FONDUTA DI CIOCCOLATO

Preparation time: 15 minutes

4 Servings

FOR THE FONDUE
1 lb. 5 oz. (600 g) **dark chocolate, chopped**
Light olive oil (if necessary)

FOR THE FRUIT
10 oz. (300 g) **strawberries**
2 **bananas**
2 **kiwifruit**

Method

In a heatproof bowl set over (not in) a pan of simmering water, melt the chocolate.

If it is too thick, dilute it by adding just enough olive oil to achieve the desired thickness.

Transfer to a fondue pot to keep warm.

Wash and hull the strawberries. Peel the bananas and the kiwifruit.

Cut the fruit into pieces and thread them onto wooden skewers, which you and your guests can then use to dip in the chocolate fondue.

Difficulty

FRUIT DESSERTS

CHAPTER SIX

APRICOT DUMPLINGS
CANEDERLI DI ALBICOCCHE

Preparation time: 30 minutes + 5 minutes cooking time

4 Servings

2 1/4 lbs. (1 kg) **russet potatoes**
9 oz. (250 g) **all-purpose flour, sifted, plus more for dusting**
3 **large eggs**
7 oz. (200 g) **unsalted butter, plus more for dough**
Salt
16 **apricots, pitted**
3/4 cup (100 g) **breadcrumbs**
1/2 cup (100 g) **sugar**
4 tbsp. (30 g) **ground cinnamon**

Method

Boil the potatoes until tender, about 15 minutes. Peel them and mash them with a ricer. Let cool. Add the flour, eggs, a pat of butter, and a pinch of salt. Turn out the dough onto a clean, lightly floured work surface and knead the dough.

Form the dough into the shape of a salami, then divide it into 6-inch-long (15 cm) pieces. Pinch off the pieces of dough and shape them into squares big enough to enclose an apricot. With floured hands, wrap an apricot in the dough, forming a ball.

Bring a large pot of salted water to a boil. Use a slotted spoon to transfer the dumplings to the pot to cook. When they float to the surface, remove them.

Meanwhile, melt the butter in a large pan. When the butter turns golden, add the breadcrumbs and cook for 1 to 2 minutes, stirring constantly.

Add the dumplings, stirring them with a wooden spoon to flavor them uniformly.

Serve hot, dusted with sugar and cinnamon.

Difficulty

CHOCOLATE-COATED FIGS
FICHI AL CIOCCOLATO

Preparation time: 20 minutes + 5 minutes cooking time

4 Servings

1 3/4 lbs. (800 g) **dried figs**
5 oz. (150 g) **almonds, toasted and chopped**
2 **cloves, crushed**
3 oz. (70 g) **candied citron**
4 oz. (100 g) **dark chocolate, grated**
1/3 cup (75 g) **sugar**
Ground cinnamon (optional)

Method

Heat the oven to 350°F (180°C).

With a sharp knife, slice into each fig from top to bottom—following the line of the stem—splitting it, but leaving the split halves still attached. Fold open each fig like a book, exposing the cut surfaces, and top each half with some of the almonds, cloves, and candied citron. Close them firmly, place on a parchment-lined baking sheet, and bake until they begin to brown, for about 5 minutes.

In a bowl, mix the chocolate and sugar. While the figs are still hot, roll them in the chocolate mixture. (Alternatively, you can melt the chocolate with a little water and a pinch of cinnamon in a baking dish, then dip the hot figs in the cinnamon-chocolate.) Place the figs on a parchment-lined baking sheet to set.

Store the chocolate-coated figs in tins or wooden boxes lined with waxed paper.

Difficulty

PEACHES IN SYRUP
PESCHE SCIROPPATE

Preparation time: 2 hours

4 Servings

2 lbs. (1 kg) **firm yellow peaches or nectarines**
2 1/2 cups (600 ml) **water**
2 cups (400 g) **sugar**
1 **vanilla bean, split lengthwise, seeds scraped**
Zest of 1 **lemon, cut into strips**
2 **cloves**

Method

Bring a large pot of water to a boil and blanch the peaches for 1 minute. Remove them with a slotted spoon and immediately place them in a bowl of ice water so the skins will be easier to remove (you can skip this step if you're using nectarines).

Cut the peaches in half, remove the pits, and place them on a clean kitchen towel to dry.

In the meantime, make the syrup. Bring the water to a boil. Add the sugar, stirring until it dissolves. Add the vanilla bean, lemon zest, and cloves. Let mixture boil for a few minutes.

Arrange the peaches in sterilized jars and pour the syrup over them. Leave 1 inch of headroom. Wipe the rims, put on the lids, and screw on the bands fingertip-tight.

Put the jars in a large pot fitted with a canning rack. Add enough water to cover the jars by 2 to 3 inches. Bring the water to a boil over high heat, then lower the heat to maintain a rolling boil. Boil the jars for 40 minutes (plus 2 minutes for every 1,000 feet above sea level). Be sure the jars are covered with water the entire time. Turn off the heat. Wait about 5 minutes and then use a jar lifter to transfer the jars to a rack or towel to cool.

Keep jars in a cool, dark, dry place. Peaches can be stored for up to 1 year.

Difficulty

APPLE FRITTERS

FRITTELLE DI MELE

Preparation time: 20 minutes + 5 minutes cooking time

10 Servings

1 cup (250 ml) **milk**
1 1/2 cups (180 g) **all-purpose flour**
2 **large eggs**
2 tbsp. (30 g) **sugar**
Salt
1 1/2 tablespoons (20 ml) **rum**
1/4 oz. (6 g) **baking powder**
4 **large Golden Delicious or Russet
    apples**
1 drop **vanilla extract**
Vegetable oil, for frying
Confectioners' sugar
Ground cinnamon (optional)

Method

Prepare a batter with the milk, flour, eggs, 1 tablespoon of sugar, a pinch of salt, vanilla extract, and the rum. To make it lighter, add the baking powder.

Peel and core the apples. Cut them into slices 1/4 inch (0.5 cm) thick.

Bring a skillet of oil to a simmer. Immerse the apple slices in the batter and fry until golden.

Serve hot, sprinkled with confectioners' sugar and a pinch of cinnamon to taste, if desired.

Difficulty

SPICY WATERMELON

COPPE D'ANGURIA

Preparation time: 15 minutes

4 Servings

1/2 **watermelon**
2 tbsp. (30 g) **sugar**
Vanilla extract
1/4 cup (60 g) **gin**
1 1/2 tbsp. (20 g) **chocolate chips**
Ground cinnamon

Method

Slice the watermelon flesh into large, thin pieces. Divide between four large dessert bowls, layering the pieces.

In a bowl, mix the sugar with a drop or two of vanilla. Sprinkle vanilla sugar over the watermelon and add a splash of gin to each portion. Refrigerate until well chilled.

To serve, sprinkle each portion with chocolate chips and cinnamon.

Difficulty

STUFFED PEACHES

PESCHE RIPIENE CON MANDORLE

Preparation time: 20 minutes + 30 minutes cooking time

4 Servings

8 peaches (not too ripe)
Unsalted butter, for baking dish
4 oz. (120 g) blanched almonds
1 roll, soaked in milk
3 large eggs, separated
3/4 cup (150 g) sugar
Confectioners' sugar, for dusting

Method

Heat the oven to 300°F (150°C).

Cut the peaches in half, and, using a sharp knife, remove and discard the pit. Remove and reserve a bit of the flesh. This also allows room for the filling. Put the peaches in a buttered baking dish, cut side up.

For the filling, crush the almonds in a mortar. Transfer to a large bowl. Press the excess milk from the roll and tear the roll into pieces. Add the pieces to the bowl with the almonds, along with the reserved peach flesh. Whisk the egg yolks with the sugar, then add the mixture to the bowl with the other ingredients. Mix all the ingredients thoroughly.

In a separate bowl, beat the egg whites until stiff peaks form. Fold them into the peach mixture.

Spoon the mixture into the cavities of the peaches and bake for about 30 minutes. Dust with confectioners' sugar and serve lukewarm.

As a variation, the almonds can be replaced with chopped macaroons.

Difficulty

CHOCOLATE-COVERED ORANGE PEELS

SCORZETTE D'ARANCIA RICOPERTE DI CIOCCOLATO

Preparation time: 12 hours

4 Servings

5 oz. (130 g) **candied orange peels**
3 oz. (70 g) **dark chocolate**

Method

Quarter the candied orange peels and place on a wire rack to dry at room temperature overnight. When orange peels are dry, cut them into strips about 1/4 inch (6 mm) wide.

Temper the dark chocolate: Melt the chocolate in a heatproof bowl set over (not in) a pan of simmering water until the chocolate reaches 110°–120°F (45°–50°C) on a candy thermometer. (Or microwave the chocolate in 15-second increments, stirring in between, until the chocolate reaches the desired temperature.) Pour one-third to one-half of the chocolate onto a marble surface or metal baking sheet set over an ice pack. Let cool until it reaches 79°–81°F (26°–27°C), then return the cooled chocolate to the remaining hot chocolate. When this mixture reaches 86°–88°F (30°–31°C), it is ready to be used.

Use a fork to dip the candied orange peels into the tempered chocolate. Drain the excess chocolate and place the coated peels on a sheet of parchment paper or waxed paper to set at room temperature.

Difficulty

ALMOND BRITTLE

CROCCANTE

Preparation time: 10 minutes + 10 minutes cooking time

10 Servings

2 tbsp. (30 ml) **water**
2 1/2 cups (500 g) **sugar**
18 oz. (500 g) **blanched almonds, chopped**
Vegetable oil, for work surface

Method

Caramelize the sugar: Heat the water and sugar in a heavy saucepan over medium-low heat, stirring only until the sugar dissolves. Bring to a boil and cook, without stirring, until the sugar is amber in color. Remove from the heat.

Add the almonds to the mixture and stir to combine. Pour the brittle onto a lightly oiled nonstick work surface (preferably marble).

Let cool undisturbed, then break the brittle into small pieces. (You can store the brittle in an airtight container for up to 10 days.)

Difficulty

ALMOND: A TRUE GASTRONOMIC PEARL

The origins of the almond are to be found in Asia Minor, as is testified by the wealth of recipes with this most fragrant of nuts. In antiquity, it was eaten all around the Mediterranean. In Italy, almonds are used to produce true gastronomic pearls, such as "confetti" (sugared almonds), biscuits, pastries, and marzipan.

CHOCOLATE-COVERED ALMONDS AND HAZELNUTS

MANDORLE E NOCCIOLE RICOPERTE DI CIOCCOLATO

Preparation time: 40 minutes

4 Servings

1 1/2 tbsp. (20 g) **sugar**
2 tsp. (10 ml) **water**
1 cup (125 g) **mixed almonds and hazelnuts**
1 tsp. (5 g) **unsalted butter**
6 oz. (180 g) **dark chocolate, melted**

Method

Put the sugar and water in a saucepan and bring to a boil.

Add the almonds and hazelnuts, then cook until the sugar becomes an amber color. Stir in the butter, then pour the mixture onto a baking sheet to cool, separating the almonds and hazelnuts.

Once the nuts have cooled, transfer them to a large bowl and add about a quarter of the chocolate. Stir so that the chocolate does not solidify, keeping the almonds and hazelnuts well separated.

Repeat until you have finished adding all of the chocolate. Transfer the chocolate-coated nuts to a large-mesh sieve set over a bowl and let the excess chocolate drain off.

Transfer the nuts to parchment and let them set. Store in a dry place at room temperature, preferably in sealed glass jars or in cans with lids.

Difficulty

SUMMER FRUIT SALAD
MACEDONIA D'ESTATE

Preparation time: 15 minutes

10 Servings

2 **melons**
3 oz. (100 g) **raspberries**
Brandy (or "passito" sweet wine)

Method

Wash the melons. Halve them lengthwise and use a spoon to remove all the seeds and fibers. Using a melon baller, scoop out the flesh, taking care not to damage the shell. Reserve the shells to use as "bowls" for the salad.

Rinse and drain the raspberries, then pat them dry with a towel.

Place the melon balls and raspberries in a bowl and toss gently with a splash of brandy or passito.

Fill the melon shells with the fruit salad; refrigerate for 30 minutes and serve.

Difficulty

THE ORIGINS OF MELON

Opinions may vary, but it is likely that melons originated from the tropical areas of Africa, where they are known to have existed before they spread to the East and on to Europe. Paintings of the fruit found in the ruins of Pompeii and Ercolano indicate that melons arrived in Europe around the first century BC.

ALPHABETICAL INDEX OF RECIPES

INGREDIENTS INDEX

All the photographs are by Alberto Rossi/ACADEMIA BARILLA except:
Chato Morandi/ACADEMIA BARILLA: pages 44, 60, 86
Lucio Rossi/ACADEMIA BARILLA: pages 64, 70, 72, 74
De Agostini Picture Library: pages 1, 232
iStockphoto: page 18

In the heart of Parma, one of the most distinguished capitals of Italian cuisine, is the Barilla Center. Set in the grounds of the former Barilla pasta factory, this modern architectural complex is the home of Academia Barilla. This was founded in 2004 to promote the art of Italian cuisine, protecting the regional gastronomic heritage and safeguarding it from imitations and counterfeits, while encouraging the great traditions of the Italian restaurant industry. Academia Barilla is also a center of great professionalism and talent that is exceptional in the world of cooking. It organizes cooking classes for culinary enthusiasts, it provides services for those involved in the restaurant industry, and it offers products of the highest quality. In 2007, Academia Barilla was awarded the "Premio Impresa-Cultura" for its campaigns promoting the culture and creativity of Italian gastronomy throughout the world. The center was designed to meet the training requirements of the world of food and it is equipped with all the multimedia facilities necessary for organizing major events. The remarkable gastronomic auditorium is surrounded by a restaurant, a laboratory for sensory analysis, and various teaching rooms equipped with the most modern technology. The Gastronomic Library contains over 11,000 books and a remarkable collection of historic menus as well as prints related to culinary subjects. The vast cultural heritage of the library can be consulted on the internet which provides access to hundreds of digitized historic texts. This avant-garde approach and the presence of a team of internationally famous experts enables Academia Barilla to offer a wide range of courses, meeting the needs of both restaurant chefs and amateur food lovers. In addition, Academia Barilla arranges cultural events and activities aiming to develop the art of cooking, supervised by experts, chefs, and food critics, that are open to the public. It also organizes the "Academia Barilla Film Award", for short films devoted to Italy's culinary traditions.

www.academiabarilla.com

METRIC EQUIVALENTS

LIQUID/DRY MEASURES	
U.S.	**METRIC**
¼ teaspoon	1.25 milliliters
½ teaspoon	2.5 milliliters
1 teaspoon	5 milliliters
1 tablespoon (3 teaspoons)	15 milliliters
1 fluid ounce (2 tablespoons)	30 milliliters
¼ cup	60 milliliters
⅓ cup	80 milliliters
½ cup	120 milliliters
1 cup	240 milliliters
1 pint (2 cups)	480 milliliters
1 quart (4 cups; 32 ounces)	960 milliliters
1 gallon (4 quarts)	3.84 liters
1 ounce (by weight)	28 grams
1 pound	454 grams
2.2 pounds	1 kilogram

OVEN TEMPERATURES

°F	GAS MARK	°C
250	½	120
275	1	140
300	2	150
325	3	165
350	4	180
375	5	190
400	6	200
425	7	220
450	8	230
475	9	240
500	10	260
550	Broil	290